Red Books *showing the way*

COUNTY STREET ATLAS

DORSET

C000245214

44 TOWN CENTRE STREET MAPS

ROAD MAPS PAGE LAYOUT

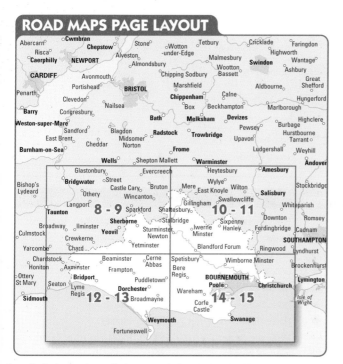

Every effort has been made to verify the accuracy of information in this book but the publishers cannot accept responsibility for expense or loss caused by an error or omission.

Information that will be of assistance to the user of the maps will be welcomed.

The representation on these maps of a road, track or path is no evidence of the existence of a right of way.

Street plans prepared and published by
Red Books (Estate Publications) Ltd, Bridewell House, Tenterden, Kent, TN30 6EP.
The Publishers acknowledge the co-operation of the local authorities of towns represented in this atlas.

Ordnance Survey® This product includes mapping data licensed from Ordnance Survey® with the permission of the Controller of Her Majesty's Stationery Office.

www.redbooks-maps.co.uk

O2007

ROAD MAPPING

1 : 200,000 - 3.16 Miles to 1 Inch

| 0 | 2 | 4 | 6 | 8 | 10 | 12 | 14 | 16 Kilometres |
| 0 | | 2 | | 4 | | 6 | | 8 | 10 Miles |

M6	Motorway	A379	'A' Road (Dual Carriageway)	Roundabouts	
23	Motorway Junction	A387	'A' Road (Single Carriageway)	National Boundary	
22	Motorway Junction (Restricted Access)	A897	Narrow 'A' Road	County Boundary	
S	Motorway Service Area	A387	'A' Road (Under Construction)	Built Up Area	
	Motorway Under Construction	B4568	'B' Road (Dual Carriageway)	Canal	
A40	Primary Route (Dual Carriageway)	B4385	'B' Road (Single Carriageway)	Lake / Reservoir & River	
A49	Primary Route (Single Carriageway)	B873	Narrow 'B' Road	Coastal Area and Beach	
S	Non Motorway Service Area		'B' Road (Under Construction)	National Scenic Area / National Park	
	Narrow Primary Route		Minor Road	Woodland	
	Primary Route (Under Construction)	●──	Railway with Station	National Trail	
6	Distance in Miles	●──	Tourist Railway with Station	12	Adjoining Pages

TOURIST SYMBOLS on road maps

✈	Airport	▦	Entertainment Centre	🏛	Prehistoric Monument
🚤	Hovercraft	❋	Garden		Roman Remains
⛴	Hydrofoil	⛳9 ⛳18	Golf Courses (9 & 18 holes)	⌇	RSPB Reserve
👥	Passenger Ferry	⚑	Golf Driving Range, Pitch & Putt		Ski Slope Centre
🚢	Seacat	◨	Holiday Centre		Sub Aqua Activity
🚢	Vehicle Ferries	🏇	Horse Racing	入	Surfing
		🏠	House / Building of Interest	🎭	Theatre
⌘	Ancient Fort	🏠	House and Garden	*i*	Tourist Information Centre
🐾	Animal Attraction	🏭	Industrial Interest	*i*	(Seasonal)
⬅	Aquarium	🎡	Leisure / Theme Park	*i*	(National Trust, National Park)
✕	Battle Site	🗼	Lighthouse		Tourist Railway
🌉	Bridge of Interest	▲	Monument, Folly	🌸	Viewpoint
⛺	Camping Site	⦿	Motorsports Centre / Venue	🍇	Vineyard & Cider Producer
⊘	Caravan Club Site	🏛	Museum / Art Gallery	⇗	Water Skiing
🚐	Caravan Site	🍁	National Nature Reserve	🏭	Watermill
🏰	Castle, Tower	⚘	National Trail	🅥	Wildlife Park
✝	Cathedral, Abbey, Priory	★	Other Place of Interest	🗙	Windmill
🏠	Church of Interest	⊕	Outdoor Pursuits	🐎	Working Farm
🏠	Country Park	⊓	Picnic Site	▲	Youth Hostel
⛴	Craft Centre	⚲	Place of Natural Beauty	🐾	Zoo

STREET MAPPING

1 : 15,840 — 4 Inches to 1 Mile

Scale: 0 — ¼ — ½ — ¾ — 1 — 1¼ — 1½ Kilometres
0 — ¼ — ½ — ¾ — 1 Mile

Legend:

- Motorway
- Primary Route
- Other 'A' Road
- 'B' Road
- Minor Road
- Pedestrianized / Restricted Access
- Track
- Footpath
- Stream
- River
- Lock / Canal
- Railway / Station
- Post Office
- P / P+ Car Park / Park & Ride
- C Public Convenience
- + Place of Worship
- → One-way Street
- i Tourist Information Centre

- Emergency Services
- Industrial Buildings
- Leisure Buildings
- Education Buildings
- Hotels etc.
- Retail Buildings
- General Buildings
- Woodland
- Orchard
- Recreational / Parkland
- Cemetery

- Built Up Area
- Area Depicting Enlarged Centre
- 23 Adjoining Pages

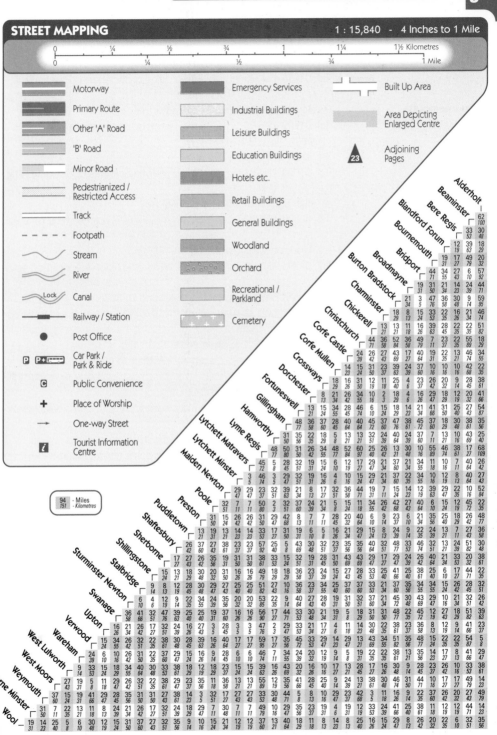

94 - Miles
151 - Kilometres

Blandford Forum 19 B5	1 Greyhound Yd, Market Pl, Blandford Forum, DT11 7EB Tel: 01258 454770 Email: blandfordtic@north-dorset.gov.uk
Bournemouth 20 C5	Westover Rd, Bournemouth, BH1 2BU Tel: 01202 451700 Email: info@bournemouth.gov.uk
Bridport 22 C4	47 South St, Bridport, DT6 3NY Tel: 01308 424901 Email: bridport.tic@westdorset-dc.gov.uk
Christchurch 28 B4	49 High St, Christchurch, BH23 1AS Tel: 01202 471780 Email: enquiries@christchurchtourism.info
Dorchester 31 E3	11 Antelope Walk, Dorchester, DT1 1BE Tel: 01305 267992 Email: dorchester.tic@westdorset-dc.gov.uk
Lyme Regis 35 E3	Guildhall Cottage, Church St, Lyme Regis, DT7 3BS Tel: 01297 442138 Email: lymeregis.tic@westdorset-dc.gov.uk
Poole Welcome Centre 38 B6	Enefco House, Poole Quay, Poole, BH15 1HJ Tel: 01202 253253 Email: info@poole.gov.uk
Shaftesbury 40 C3	8 Bell St, Shaftesbury, SP7 8AE Tel: 01747 853514 Email: shaftesburytic@north-dorset.gov.uk
Sherborne 41 D3	3 Tilton Ct, Digby Rd, Sherborne, DT9 3NL Tel: 01935 815341 Email: sherborne.tic@westdorset-dc.gov.uk
Swanage 45 G4	The White House, Shore Rd, Swanage, BH19 1LB Tel: 01929 422885 Email: mail@swanage.gov.uk
Wareham 50 B6	Holy Trinity Church, South St, Wareham, BH20 4LU Tel: 01929 552740 Email: tic@purbeck-dc.gov.uk
Weymouth & Portland 55 F1	The King's Statue, The Esplanade, Weymouth, DT4 7AN Tel: 01305 785747 Email: tic@weymouth.gov.uk
Wimborne Minster 57 B3	29 High St, Wimborne Minster, BH21 1HR Tel: 01202 886116 Email: wimbornetic@eastdorset.gov.uk

This COUNTY STREET ATLAS contains street maps for each town centre.
The street atlases listed below are LOCAL STREET ATLASES,
with comprehensive local coverage.

BOURNEMOUTH

including: Barton on Sea, Bearwood, Boscombe, Bransgore, Burton, Christchurch,
Everton, Ferndown, Hamworthey, Highcliffe, Hordle, Merley, Milford on Sea,
Mudeford, New Milton, Poole, Ringwood, St Ives, St Leonards, Sandbanks,
Sway, Upton, Verwood, West Moors, Wimborne Minster etc.

NEW FOREST

including: Ashurst, Barton on Sea, Beaulieu, Bransgore, Brockenhurst, Burley, Cadnam,
Christchurch, Dibden Purlieu, Everton, Fawley, Fordingbridge,
Hammonds Green, Highcliffe, Hordle, Hythe, Lymington, Lyndhurst,
Milford on Sea, Mudeford, New Milton, Ringwood, Sway, Totton etc.

WEYMOUTH & DORCHESTER

including: Broadmayne, Charlestown, Charminster, Chickerell, Crossways, Dorchester,
Easton, Fortuneswell, Martinstown, Preston, Puddletown, Radipole,
Southlands, Southwell, Upwey, West Stafford, Wyke Regis etc.

For a complete title listing please visit our website
www.redbooks-maps.co.uk

Huntworth Westonzoyland Alhampton Bruton Hardway

North Middlezoy Henley Compton Southwood Ansford Cole Pitcombe Redlynch
etherton Dundon Wootton Butleigh East Alford Castle Shepton Penselwood
oxton Northmoor Baltonsborough Ham Hornblotton Sutton Cary Montague Charlton
akton North Green Othery High Ham St. David West Lydford Lovington Galhampton Bratton Musgrove Leigh
nfield Newton Burrowbridge Kingweston Littleton Keinton Seymour Common Stoke
Creech Hedging Lyng Stathe Aller Low Ham Mandeville North Yarlington **Wincanton** Trister
St. Michael Meare Stoke Pitney **Somerton** Babcary Barrow North Cucklington
Ruishton Knapp Green St. Gregory **Langport** **Huish** **Charlton** Charlton Cadbury Holton Lattiford
Ham **North** Curry Drayton **Episcopi** **Mackrell** Adam South Compton Nth.
Thornfalcon **Curry** Rivel Muchelney Long Kingsdon Queen Cadbury Pauncefoot Cheriton Buckho
West Wrantage Fivehead Sutton Podimore Camel Sutton Charlton Sth. Westo
Hatch Curry Isle Hambridge **Kingsbury** Stapleton West Montis Horethorne Cheriton Templecombe Fife
Beer Mallet Brewers **Episcopi** Long Camel Marston Corton Combe Horsington Mag
Crocombe Isle Load **Ilchester** Yeovilton Chilton Magna Denham Stowell Yenston
Curland Ashill Abbotts Westport East Ash Limington Cantelo Rimpton Poyntington Milborne Henstridge
Ilton Lambrook Barrington **Martock** **Tintinhull** Yeovil Mudford Adber Sandford Wick Milborne
Windmill Puckington Chilthorne Marsh Trent Orcas Oborne Port Stalbridge
Blackwater Broadway Horton Shepton **South** Domer Nether Goathill Stalbridge
sland Beauchamp **Petherton** **Stoke Sub** Montacute Compton North Haydon Weston
Mary **Ilminster** Seavington Over **Hamdon** **Yeovil** Wootton Stourton Bishop's
Donyatt Kingstone St. Michael Stratton Norton Odcombe Alweston Caundle Caundle Lydlinch
Combe Dowlish Seavington Lopen Sub Hamdon Chiselborough **Bradford** Thornford Folke
St. Nicholas Wake St. Mary **Merriott** West Chinnock **Abbas** Beer Lillington Longburton
testaunton Cudworth Dinnington Hinton West East **West** East Stoford Hackett King's
Wadeford Chillington St. George **Crewkerne** Chinnock Chinnock **Coker** Coker Ryme **Yetminster** Stag King
Chaffcombe Haselbury Hardington Intrinseca Holwell Hazelbury
Wambrook **Chard** Cricket Hewish North Plucknett Mandeville Leigh Glanvilles Bryan Wonston
St. Thomas Misterton Perrott Halstock Holnest Wootton Pulham Mappowder
Forton Wayford Clapton South Melbury Chetnole Hermitage Middlemarsh Duntish
Tatworth Winsham Seaborough Perrott Osmond Melbury **D**
Furley South Drimpton Mosterton Chedington Corscombe Chelborough Sampford Melbury Lyon's Buckland Melcomb
Chardstock Chard Evershot Bubb Gate Newton Bingham
mbury Thorncombe Burstock **Broadwindsor** **WEST** **DORSET** Holywell Batcombe Minterne Alton Plush
Churchill Holditch Toller Rampisham Frome Magna Pancras
od Smallridge Hawkchurch Birdsmoorgate **Beaminster** Whelme St. Quintin Up Cerne Piddletrenthide Cheselbou
Kilmington Bettiscombe Stoke Hooke Wraxall Up Cerne White
Axminster Marshwood Pilsdon Abbott Mapperton Lower Cattistock Sydling Nether Lackington
Musbury Wootton **Netherbury** Melplash Kingcombe Chilfrome St. Nicholas Cerne Piddlehinton
Fitzpaine Broadoak Waytown Poorton Toller **Maiden** Godmanstone
Uplyme Whitchurch Salwayash Melbury West Porcorum **Newton** Forston
Combpyne Morcombelake Canonicorum North Milton Powerstock Toller Wynford
Charmouth Ryall Chideock Nettlecombe Fratrum Eagle Frampton Stratton **Charminster** Puddl
Axmouth Rousdon **Symondsbury** **Bridport** Bradpole Loders West Grimstone **Dorchester**
Lyme Regis Chideock Uploders Askerswell Compton Compton Bradford Peverell
Seatown Waldditch Shipton Kingston Valence Poundbury Stinsford Tinc
Eype **Bothenhampton** Gorge Russell Winterbourne Bockhampton
West Bay Litton Long Abbas West
Chilcombe Cheney Bredy Winterbourne Stafford Crossw
Burton Litttlebredy Steepleton Martinstown Winterborne West
Bradstock Swyre Punknowle Monkton Winterborne Knighton
West Herringston **Broadmayne** Owe
Bexington Abbotsbury Portesham Bincombe
Rodden Upwey **Preston** Poxw
Chickerell **WEYMOUTH** Broadwey Osmington
Langton **& PORTLAND** Nottington Osmingt
Herring Radipole Mills
Charlestown **Weymouth**
Wyke Southlands
Regis
Fortuneswell
Grove
Weston Easton
Southwell

Chicklade
Great Wishford
Stoford Woodford
Lower Woodford
Winterbourne Dauntsey
Winterbourne Gunner

Berwick St. Leonard
Fonthill Bishop
South Newton
Winterbourne Earls
Middle Winterslow

Mere
West Knoyle
Hindon
Chilmark
Teffont Magna
Dinton
Baverstock
Wilton
Bemerton Heath
Firsdown
West Winterslow
The Common

The Green
East Knoyle
Fonthill Gifford
Ridge
Teffont Evias
Chicksgrove
Barford St. Martin
Burcombe
Quidhampton
Laverstock
Pitton
West Tytherley

Barrow Street
Tisbury
Newtown
Hatch
Sutton Mandeville
Fovant
Compton Chamberlayne
Netherhampton
Harnham
Salisbury
Farley
East Grimstead
West Dean

Milton on Stour
Gillingham
Sedgehill
Semley
Swallowcliffe
Coombe Bissett
Stratford Tony
Britford
Odstock
Homington
Nunton
Alderbury
Whaddon
Bodenham
West Grimstead
East Dean

Motcombe
Donhead St. Mary
Donhead St. Andrew
Broad Chalke
Bishopstone
Charlton-All-Saints
Whiteparish

Shaftesbury
Ludwell
Ebbesbourne Wake
Bowerchalke

East Stour
Cann Common
Charlton
Berwick St. John
Alvediston
Woodminton
Wick
Downton
Morgan's Vale
Redlynch
Sherfield English
Landford Manor

Stour Row
Guy's Marsh
Cann
Melbury Abbas
Martin Drove End
Woodfalls
Lover

Todber
Compton Abbas
Ashmore
Tollard Royal
Deanland
Woodyates
Martin
Tidpit
Whitsbury
Rockbourne
Upper Street
Breamore
Nth. Charford
Hale
Woodgreen
Landford
Plaitford
Canada

Margaret Marsh
West Orchard
Fontmell Magna
Sixpenny Handley
Pentridge
Damerham
Nomansland
Bramshaw

Manston
Sutton Waldron
Farnham
Dean
Fordingbridge
Godshill

NORTH DORSET
Hammoon
Iwerne Minster
Stubhampton
Chettle
Cashmoor
Monkton Up Wimborne
Sandleheath
Cranborne
Stuckton
Blissford
Fritham
Brook

Fiddleford
Child Okeford
Iwerne Courtney or Shroton
Tarrant Gunville
Tarrant Hinton
Gussage St. Michael
Wimborne St Giles
Edmondsham
Alderholt
Bickton
Hyde
North Gorley
Stoney Cross

Shillingstone
Stourpaine
Tarrant Launceston
Long Crichel
Gussage All Saints
EAST DORSET
South Gorley

Durweston
Pimperne
Tarrant Monkton
More Crichel
Woodlands
Verwood
Ibsley
Mockbeggar
Linwood
Emery Down

Turnworth
Blandford Camp
Manswood
Horton
Chalbury Common
Wigbeth
Blashford
Linford
Picket Post

Blandford Forum
Bryanston
Tarrant Rawston
Witchampton
Hinton Martell
Three Legged Cross
Ringwood
Burley Street

Winterborne Stickland
Blandford St. Mary
Tarrant Keyneston
Tarrant Rushton
Gaunt's Common
Mannington
Ashley Heath
St Ives
Avon Castle
Burley
Bisterne Close

Houghton
D O R S E T
Charlton Marshall
Tarrant Crawford
Stanbridge
Holt
West Moors
St Leonards
Kingston
Brockenhurst

Milton Abbas
Winterborne Clenston
Thorncombe
Spetisbury
Shapwick
Tadden
Clapgate
Broom Hill
Colehill
Stapehill
Trickett's Cross

Whatcombe
Winterborne Whitechurch
Almer
Sturminster Marshall
Wimborne Minster
Hampreston
West Parley
Parley Cross
Ferndown
Avon
Thorney Hill
Ripley
Bransgore
Sway
Wootton

Milborne St. Andrew
Winterborne Zelston
Anderson
East End
Merley
Longham
Hurn
Sopley
Neacroft
New Milton
Bashley

Turners Puddle
Bere Regis
Winterborne Kingston
West Morden
East Morden
Corfe Mullen
Broadstone
Bearwood
Ensbury
Burton
Hinton
Highcliffe

Bloxworth
Lytchett Matravers
Upton
Waterloo
Moordown
Mudeford
Barton on Sea

Briantspuddle
Lytchett Minster
Slepe
Newtown
Winton
POOLE
BOURNEMOUTH
Christchurch
Milford on Sea

Holton Heath
Hamworthy
Branksome
Westbourne
Boscombe
Southbourne

PURBECK
Sandford
Bonkley Sands
Poole
Parkstone
Branksome Park
Bournemouth

Bovington Camp
Wareham
Arne

East Burton
Stokeford
Sandbank

East Knighton
Wool
East Stoke
Stoborough
Ridge

Winfrith Newburgh
Coombe Keynes
West Holme
Stoborough Green
Norden

Herringstaidon
East Lulworth
Furzebrook
East Creech
Studland

West Lulworth
Corfe Castle

Tyneham
Steeple
Church Knowle
Kingston
Harman's Cross
Langton Matravers
Swanage

Kimmeridge
Worth Matravers

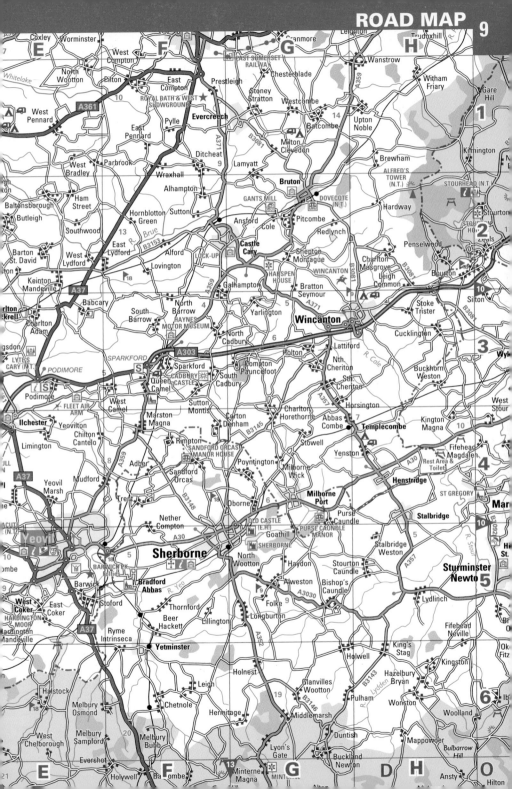

E   F   G   H

Coxley   Worminster   West   Leighton   Trudoxhill
Compton   EAST SOMERSET   Cranmore   Wanstrow   Witham
North   RAILWAY   Chesterblade   Friary   Gare
Wootton   Pilton   East   Prestleigh   Stoney   Hill
West Compton   Compton   Stratton   Westcombe   Upton   Kilmington
Pennard   ROYAL BATH & WEST   Evercreech   Milton   Batcombe   Noble   STOURHEAD (N.T.)
SHOWGROUND   Pylle   Clevedon   ALFRED'S
West   East   Ditcheat   Lamyatt   TOWER
Bradley   Parbrook   Pennard   Wraxhall   Bruton   Brewham   (N.T.)   Stourton
West   Ham   Alhampton   GANTS MILL   Hardway   Penselwood
Baltonsborough   Street   Hornblotton   Sutton   Ansford   DOVECOTE   Bourton   Stourton
Butleigh   Green   Cole   Pitcombe   (N.T.)
Southwood   East   Alford   Castle   Redlynch   Silton
West   Lydford   Lovington   Cary   Shepton   Charlton   Penselwood
Barton   West   LOCK-UP   Montague   Masgrove
St. David   Lydford   Galhampton   HANSPEN   WINCANTON   Leigh
Keinton   Babcary   North   HOUSE   Bratton   Common   Stoke
Mandeville   South   Barrow   Yarlington   Seymour   Trister
Charlton   Barrow   HAYNES   Wincanton   Cucklington
Adam   MOTOR MUSEUM   North   Lattiford   Buckhorn
SPARKFORD   Cadbury   Holton   Nth   Weston   West
LYTES   Sparkford   Compton   Cheriton   Stour
CARY (N.T.)   PODIMORE   South   Pauncefoot   Sth
Podimore   Queen   CADBURY   Cadbury   Cheriton   Horsington   Kington
FLEET AIR   Camel   CASTLE   Sutton   Charlton   Abbas   Magna
ARM   West   Montis   Horethorne   Combe   Templecombe   Fifehead
Ilchester   Yeovilton   Camel   Marston   Corton   Stowell   Yenston   Magdalen
Limington   Chilton   Magna   Denham   Charlton   Rest Area &
Cantelo   Rimpton   SANDFORD ORCAS   Horethorne   Milborne   Toilets
Mudford   Adber   MANOR HOUSE   Poyntington   Wick   Henstridge   ST GREGORY
Yeovil   Sandford   Milborne   Mar
Marsh   Trent   Orcas   Oborne   Port   Purse   Stalbridge
Nether   OLD CASTLE   Caundle   PURSE CAUNDLE   St.
Yeovil   Compton   (E.H.)   Goathill   MANOR   Stalbridge
SHERBORNE   Weston   Sturminster
BARWICK PK   Sherborne   North   Haydon   Stourton   Newton
Barwick   Wootton   Caundle   Bishop's
Bradford   Alweston   Caundle   Lydlinch
West   East   Abbas   Stoford   Folke   A3030   King's   Fifehead
Coker   Coker   Thornford   Longburton   Stag   Néville
HARBINGTON   Beer   Lillington   Holwell   Kingston
MOOR   Ryme   Hackett   Holnest   Hazelbury
Mandeville   Intrinseca   Yetminster   Bryan   Wonston   Woolland
Leigh   Glanvilles   Pulham   Mappowder
Halstock   Melbury   Chetnole   Wootton   Middlemarsh   Duntish   Bulbarrow
Osmond   Hermitage   Hill
West   Melbury   Melbury   Lyon's   Buckland   Ansty
Chelborough   Sampford   Bubb   Evershot   Holywell   Gate   Newton   Hilton
Minterne   MINT.
Magna

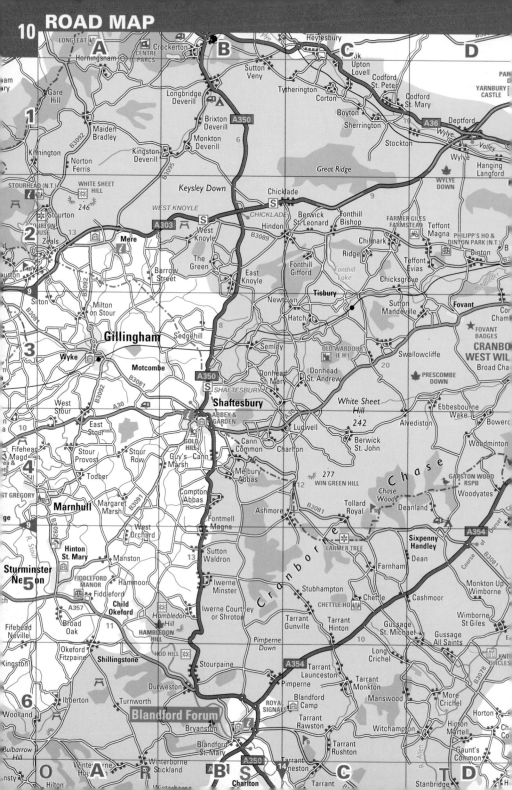

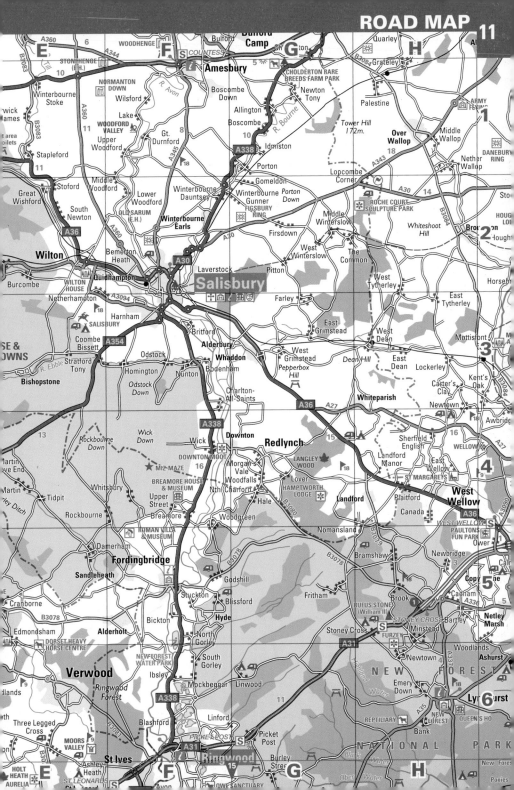

E **F** **G** **H**

MOORS VALLEY 9

St Ives
Ashley Heath
ST LEONARD'S
St Leonards
HOLT HEATH
AURELIA
West Moors
Stapehill
STAPEHILL ABBEY
KNOLL
West Parley
Ensbury

Ferndown
Parley Cross
Trickett's Cross
MATCHAMS
A338
AVON HEATH
Avon Castle
Kingston
CHRISTCHURCH SKI CENTRE

Moors

A31
A348
Winton
A3060
A3049
BOURNEMOUTH
Westbourne
Boscombe
Southbourne
CLIFF LIFTS
SHELL HOUSE

BOURNEMOUTH INTERNATIONAL
Hurn
ALICE IN WONDERLAND
A338
FORD BRIDGE

Bournemouth
Canford Cliffs

Ring wood 11
A31
OWL SANCTUARY
Burley
KINGSTON GREAT COMMON
9
Thorney Hill
Avon
Ripley
Sopley
Neacroft
Bransgore
Hinton
Burton
Highcliffe
Mudeford
HIGHCLIFFE
Hengistbury Head

Burley Street
Bisterne Close

PICKET'S POST
Picket Post
Black Water
NATIONAL P
Ober Water
New Fores
Ponies
Balmerlawn
Brockenhurst
Setley
13
SWAY
Sway
Battramsley
Wootton
Bashley
SAMMY MILLER
B3055
A35
B3058
New Milton
A337
Hordle
10
Downton
Everton
CHEWTON GLEN
Barton on Sea
18
Lymore
Lower Penning
BRAXTON
Keyhaven

Christchurch

Milford on Sea

HURST
Colwell Bay
Totland
Totland Bay

Totland

P O O L E   B A Y

POOLE TO:
JERSEY, GUERNSEY,
ST MALO, CHERBOURG

Alum Bay
THE NEEDLES PARK
The Needles
THE NEEDLES OLD BATTERY (N.T.)
DIMB LOD

The Foreland or Handfast Pt.

d Pt.

ge Bay

age

ead

Christchurch Bay
Christchurch Bay

1
2
3
4
5
6

E **F** **G** **H**

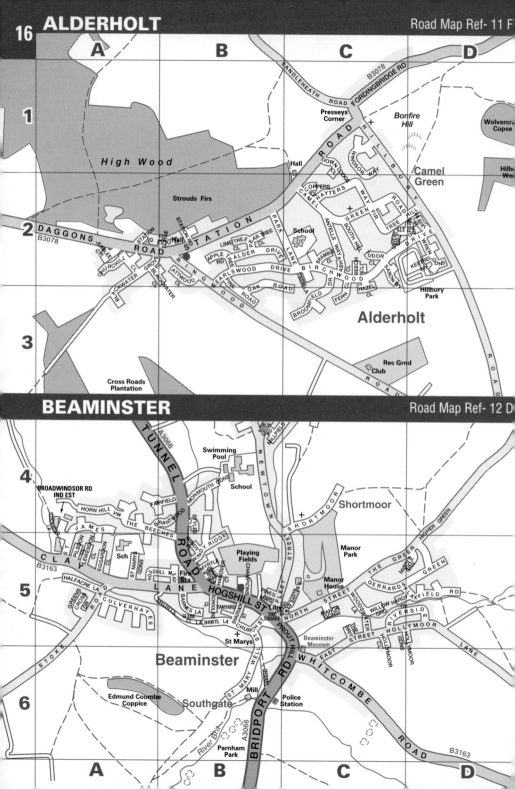

A **B** **C** **D**

1

High Wood

Strouds Firs

SANDLEHEATH ROAD

FORDINGBRIDGE RD

B3078

Presseys Corner

Bonfire Hill

Wolvercr Copse

Camel Green

Hilb Wo

Hall

ROAD

HILLBURY

DOWN LODGE

WINDSOR WAY

COPPERS

HAYTERS

CAMEL

WAY

FIR

WAY

SOUTH HILL

GREEN

TREE

ROAD

GREEN HILL

DRIVE

WREN CL

2 DAGGONS
B3078

STATION

EDGE

STATION

STATION RD

RING WOOD

ROAD

Hall

ATTWOOD

BLACKWATER

BLCKWATER CL

CHURCHILL CL

GROVE

LIME TREE CL

PEAR TREE

APPLE TREE

ALDER CL

PINE RD

EARLSWOOD DRIVE

OAK ROAD

BROOMFIELD

PARK LANE

DRIVE

BIRCH

BRAMBLE

ANTELLS WAY

HSY WAY

HYSWOOD

BEECH CL

FERN CL

HAZEL CL

TUDOR CL

SAXON WAY

BEECH CL

KESTREL CL

School

Alderholt

Hillbury Park

3

Cross Roads Plantation

Rec Grnd

Club

ROAD

ROAD

TUNNEL

A3066

BOWL GROVE

MILLFIELD

NEWTOWN

Swimming Pool

School

BROADWINDSOR RD
IND EST

HORN HILL

FAIRFIELD

MONMOUTH GDNS

BRANTWOOD

Shortmoor

SHORTMOOR

STREET

Shortmoor

4

THE BEECHES

JAMES

PILSDON

LEWESDON

EGGARDON

ROAD

LANE

Sch

HOSHILL MEAD

WINDY RIDGE

MYRTLE

HANOVER

CHAMPIONS CL

Playing Fields

Manor Park

THE GREEN

HIGHER GREEN

MIDDLE LANE

GERRARDS

GREEN

RD

CLAY
B3163

HALFACRE LA

GREENS CROSS

ROAD

CULVERHAYES

ST MARYS GDNS

HOGSHILL ST

Fire Sta

BARNES LA

GLEBE

SHORTS LA

SHORTS LA

PINES MWS

HOLLYWATER GRO

NORTH STREET

WILLOW

WOODSWATER

HARDY AXFIELD

RD

RIVERSID

HOLLYMOOR

5

Library

THE SQUARE

P

MWS

Manor House

MANOR GDNS

THE BRIT

HOLLYMOOR

GDNS

STOKE ROAD

St Marys

CHURCH ST

Beaminster Museum

EAST STREET

WHITCOMBE

HOLLYMOOR LANE

Beaminster

ST MARY WELL ST

PROUT HILL RD

BRIDPORT RD

ROAD

B3163

6

Edmund Coombe Coppice

Southgate

Mill

Police Station

Parnham Park

A3066

River Bri

A **B** **C** **D**

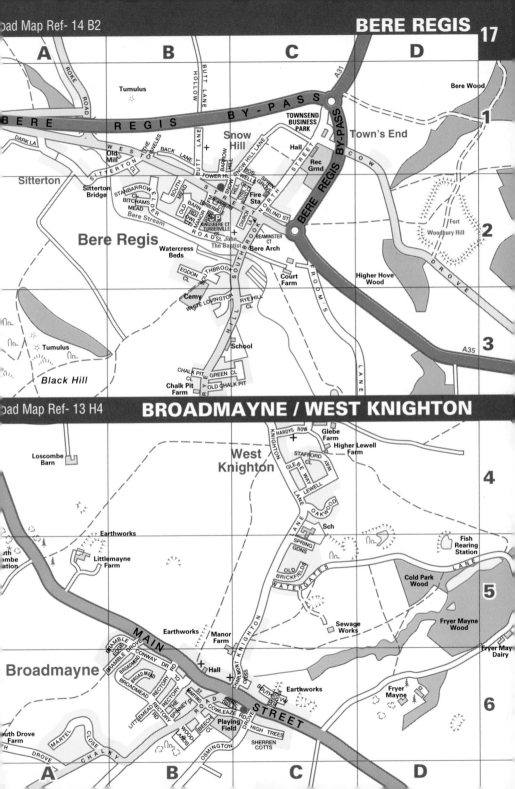

A   B   C   D

BERE WOOD

Tumulus

BERE REGIS BY-PASS

TOWNSEND BUSINESS PARK

Town's End

Snow Hill

Hall

Rec Grnd

Sitterton

Old Mill

Sitterton Bridge

STANBARROW CL

BITCHAMS MEAD

Bere Stream

Bere Regis

Fire Sta

BLIND ST

BERE REGIS BY-PASS

Fort

Woodbury Hill

DROVE

KINGSBERE CT

TURBERVILLE

St. John
The Baptist

BEAMINSTER CT

Bere Arch

Watercress Beds

EGDON CL

SOUTHBROOK CL

Court Farm

FROOM'S

Higher Hove Wood

A35

Cemy

WHITE LOVINGTON CL

RYE HILL CL

School

Tumulus

Black Hill

CHALK PIT CL

GREEN CL

Chalk Pit Farm

OLD CHALK PIT

LANE

A31

Loscombe Barn

HARDYS ROW

Glebe Farm

Higher Lewell Farm

West Knighton

STAFFORD AVY

GLEBE WAY

LEWELL

KNIGHTON LANE

OAKWOOD

Sch

Fish Rearing Station

Earthworks

Littlemayne Farm

SPRING GDNS

OLD BRICKFIELDS

WATERGATES

Cold Park Wood

LANE

Fryer Mayne Wood

Earthworks

Manor Farm

KNIGHTON

Sewage Works

Fryer Mayne Dairy

Broadmayne

MAIN

BRAMBLE EDGE

BRAMBLE DROVE

CONWAY DR

BROADMEAD RD

RECTORY RD

Hall

CHARLMONT CROSS

Fryer Mayne

STREET

LITTLEMEAD RECTORY RD

ST MARTINS RD

THE SPINNEY

COWLEAZE DROVE

SOUTHVW

Earthworks

South Drove Farm

MARTEL CLOSE

CHALKY DROVE

BEECH WOOD LANE

OSMINGTON DROVE

Playing Field

HIGH TREES

SHERREN COTTS

A   B   C   D

1   2   3   4   5   6

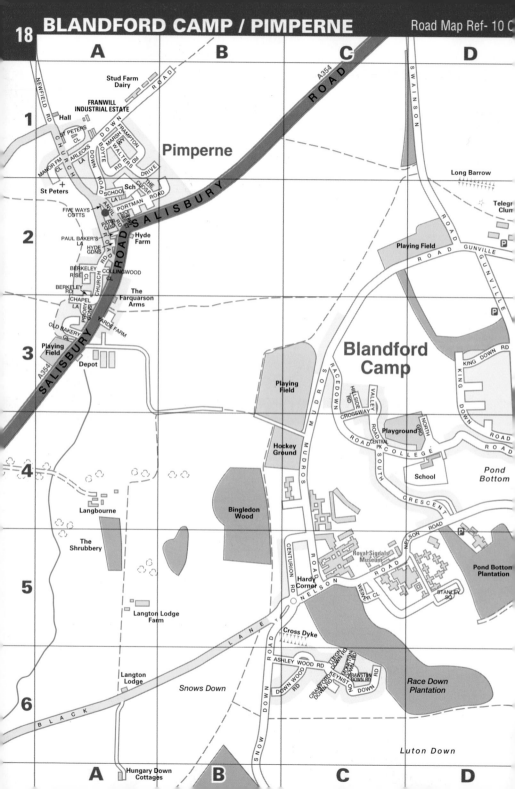

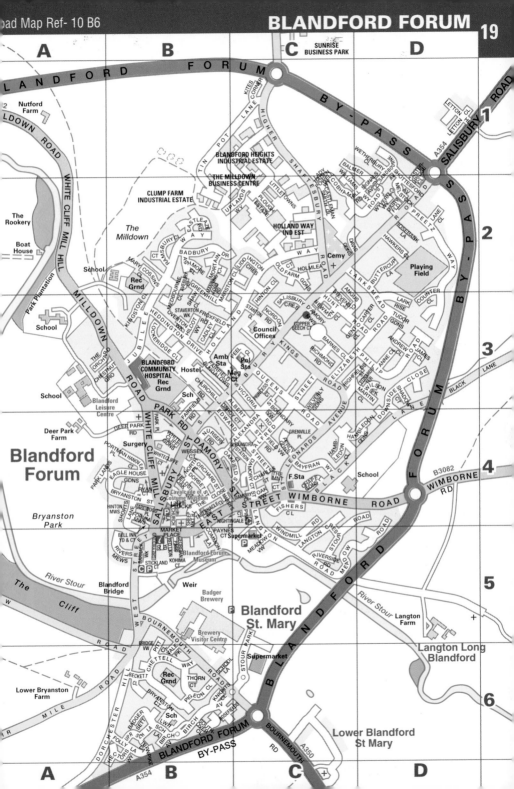

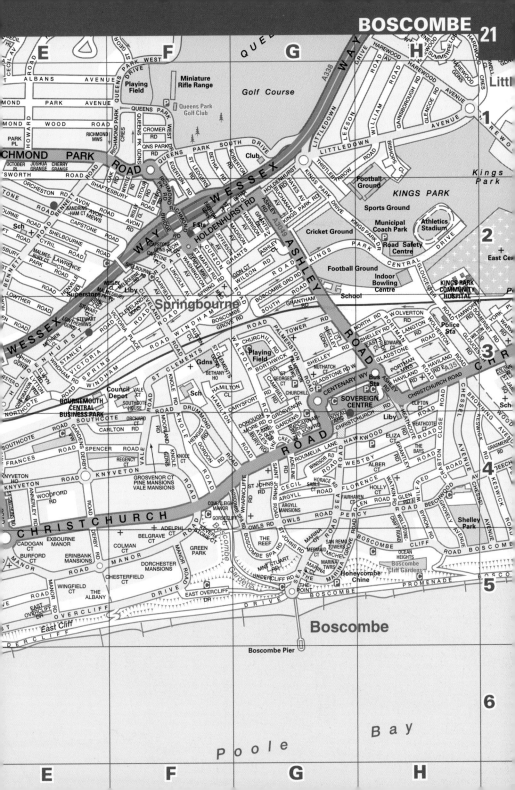

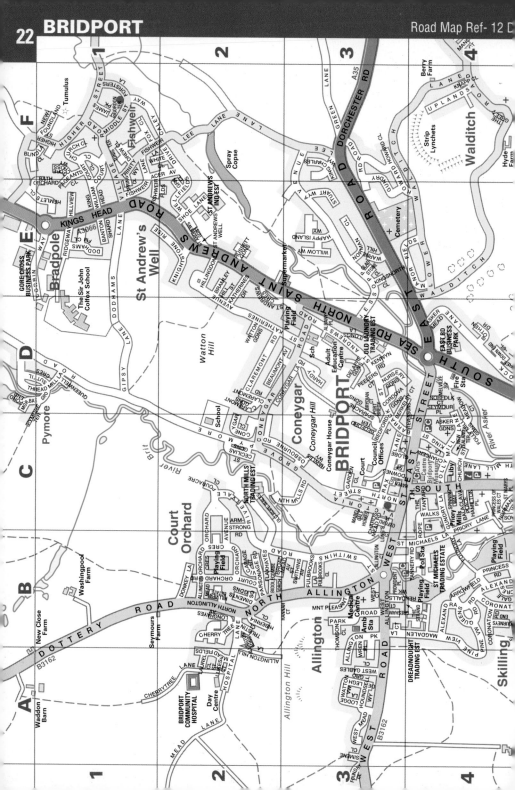

Grid references: 5, 6, 7, 8 (top); A, B, C, D, E, F (right margin); 5, 6, 7, 8 (bottom)

Hyde Hill, Sadness Copse, The Warren, Strip Lynchets, Barretts Copse, Pitfold Farm, Hyde Plantation, Bottom Wood, Bothenhampton, Holy Trinity Church (Remains of), Middlehill Farm, Little Wych, Marsh Barton Farm, Bridport & West Dorset Golf Club, Golf Course, B3157, Wych Farm, Westtown, West Bay, River Brit, Supermarket, Brewery, South Bridge, Football Grnd, Sch, Sports Ground, Bridport Leisure Centre, Broomhills Farm, Camping & Caravan Park, Bridport Arms Hotel, Old Shipyard Centre, Esplanade, Watton Cross, Watton, Watton Farm, Westcliff Farm, Chesil Beach, South West Coast Path

Road names include: BRIDPORT BY-PASS, A35, SEA ROAD, BURTON ROAD, BAY ROAD WEST, WEST BAY ROAD, WANDERWELL, BROAD, WATTON LANE, SKILLING HILL ROAD, VALLEY RD, OLD CHURCH RD, MARROWBONE LA, GREEN LANE, CROCK LANE, BOWHAYES, ELWELL, PASTURE WAY, MAPLE GARDENS, SLADES GRN, HOLLOW WAY, MEECH, NORTH HILL, WYCH HILL, MARSH GATE, WYCHSIDE, FOXGLOVE WAY, BUTTERCUP WAY, POPPY WAY, BRAMBLE, MEADOWLANDS, SEAWARD GDNS, QUAYSIDE, STATION RD, PIER TER, GEORGE, HERON CT, WESTPOINT CT, MEADWAY, CLIFF RISE, WEST WALK, BRIT VIEW RD, WEST, FOURTH WK, THIRD WK, SECOND WK, FIRST WK

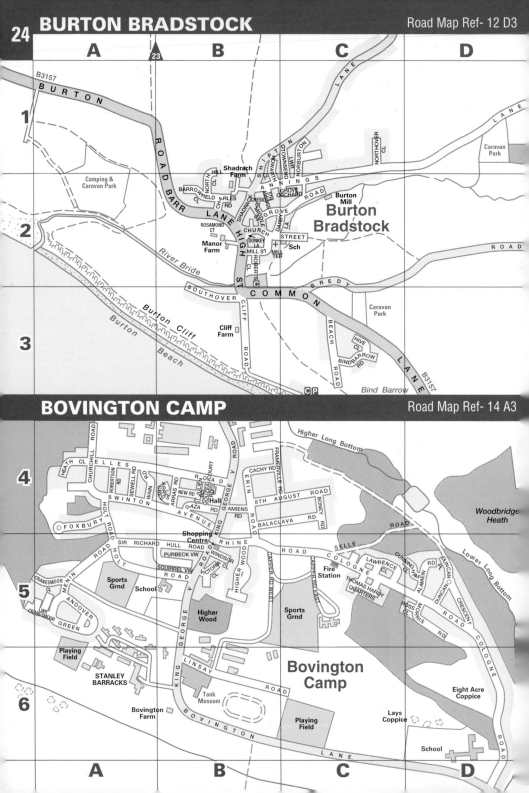

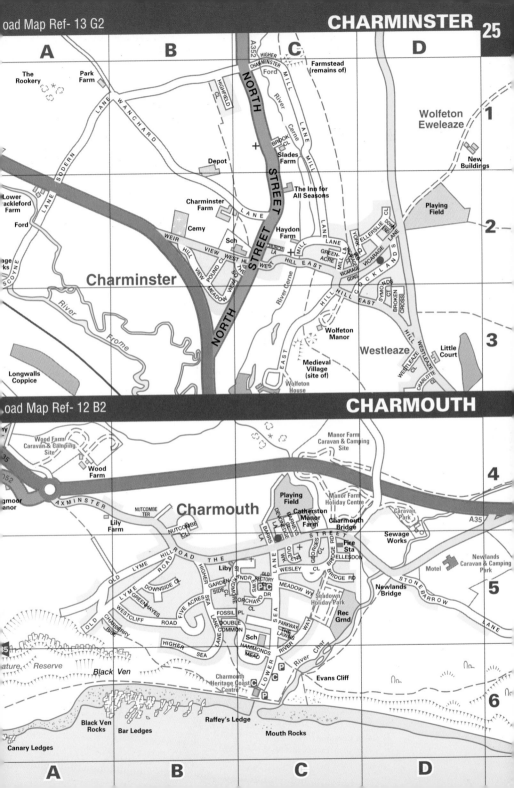

A | B | C | D

1

The Rookery

Park Farm

HIGHFIELD

HIGHER CHARMINSTER

Ford

River Cerne

MILL LANE

NORTH STREET

Farmstead (remains of)

Wolfeton Eweleaze

LANE

WANCHARD

SODERN LANE

Depot

BROOK CL

Slades Farm

New Buildings

2

Lower ackleford Farm

Ford

ge ks

SCOYNE

LANE

Charminster Farm

Cemy

WEIR HILL

Sch

VIEW

WEST VIEW

POUND CL

MEADOW VIEW

SCOYNE

THE VIEW

LANE

CHURCH

WEST HILL EAST

GREEN-ACRE

Haydon Farm

MILL HILL

MILL LA

VICARAGE GDNS

VICARAGE

YORK PL

ELLERSLIE CL

DORI

DOCKLANDS

SYMONDS CT

BROKEN CROSS

LANE

Playing Field

Little Court

Charminster

River Cerne

EAST HILL

HILL EAST

WESTLEAZE CL

CHARLOTTE CL

WESTLEAZE

3

River Frome

Longwalls Coppice

Wolfeton Manor

Medieval Village (site of)

Wolfeton House

Westleaze

ry

Wood Farm Caravan & Camping Site

35

Wood Farm

Manor Farm Caravan & Camping Site

AXMINSTER

4

gmoor anor

Lily Farm

NUTCOMBE TER

NUTCOMBE CL

Charmouth

Playing Field

BARNEY'S LA

DEVONEDGE LA

Catherston Manor Farm

Manor Farm Holiday Centre

Charmouth Bridge

Caravan Park

A35

Sewage Works

5

HILL ROAD

OLD LYME ROAD

HIGHER

GARDEN SIDE

THE SEA

STONMORE

Liby

OLD RECTORY

PTC

ORCHARD

WNDR

MEADOW WY

WESLEY CL

BRIDGE RD

BARRS LA

QUEENS

GEORGES WK

STREET

ELLESDON

BRIDGE RD

Fire Sta

Newlands Bridge

STONE BARROW

Motel

Newlands Caravan & Camping Park

LYME

DOWNSIDE CL

GREENHAYES

WESTCLIFF ROAD

FOSSIL PL

LANE

DOUBLE COMMON

Seadown Holiday Park

Rec Grnd

PARKWAY

THE LAWNS

LANE

FIVE ACRES

OLD CHARBERRY RISE

HIGHER SEA LANE

Sch

HAMMONDS MEAD

LOWER SEA LANE

WAY

River Chat

6

ature. Reserve

Black Ven

Charmouth Heritage Coast Centre

Evans Cliff

Black Ven Rocks

Bar Ledges

Raffey's Ledge

Mouth Rocks

Canary Ledges

A | B | C | D

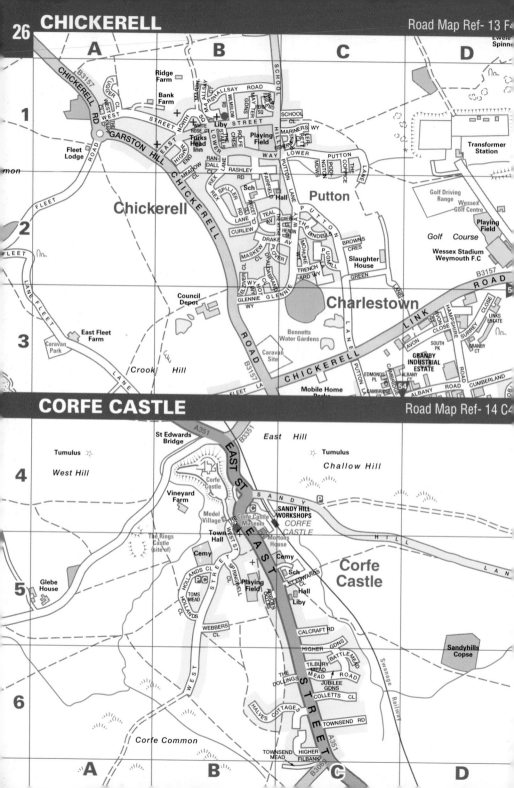

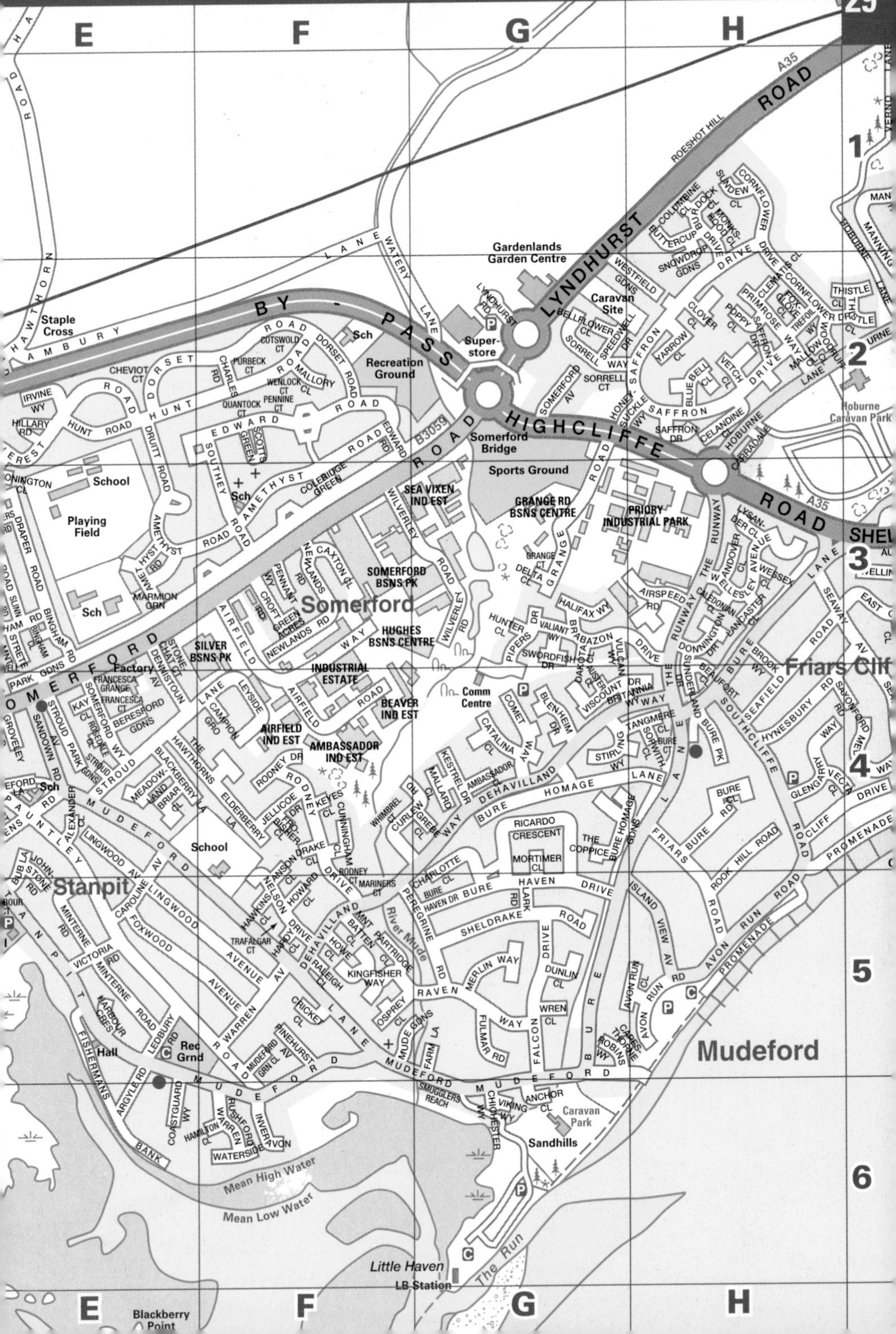
E
F
G
H
1
2
3
4
5
6
A35
ROAD
LYNDHURST
ROESHOT HILL
BY - PASS
HIGHCLIFFE
B3059
ROAD
WATERY LANE
LANE
Staple Cross
HAWTHORN ROAD
AMBURY
Gardenlands Garden Centre
Caravan Site
Super-store
Sch
Recreation Ground
Somerford Bridge
Sports Ground
School
Playing Field
Sch
Sch
SEA VIXEN IND EST
GRANGE RD BSNS CENTRE
PRIORY INDUSTRIAL PARK
SOMERFORD BSNS PK
Somerford
HUGHES BSNS CENTRE
SILVER BSNS PK
INDUSTRIAL ESTATE
BEAVER IND EST
AIRFIELD IND EST
AMBASSADOR IND EST
Factory
Comm Centre
Friars Cliff
School
Stanpit
Hoburne Caravan Park
Rec Grnd
Hall
Mudeford
Caravan Park
Sandhills
River Mude
Mean High Water
Mean Low Water
Little Haven
LB Station
The Run
Blackberry Point
SOMERFORD
MUDEFORD
STANPIT
PROMENADE
AVON RUN RD
BURE LANE
BURE HOMAGE LANE
DEHAVILLAND
FRIARS CLIFF DRIVE
SOUTHCLIFFE
SAFFRON
CORNFLOWER DRIVE
HOBURNE LANE
DORSET ROAD
HUNT ROAD
EDWARD ROAD
AMETHYST ROAD
DRUITT ROAD
SOUTHEY ROAD
WILVERLEY ROAD
AIRFIELD WAY
AIRFIELD ROAD
GRANGE ROAD
SEAWAY

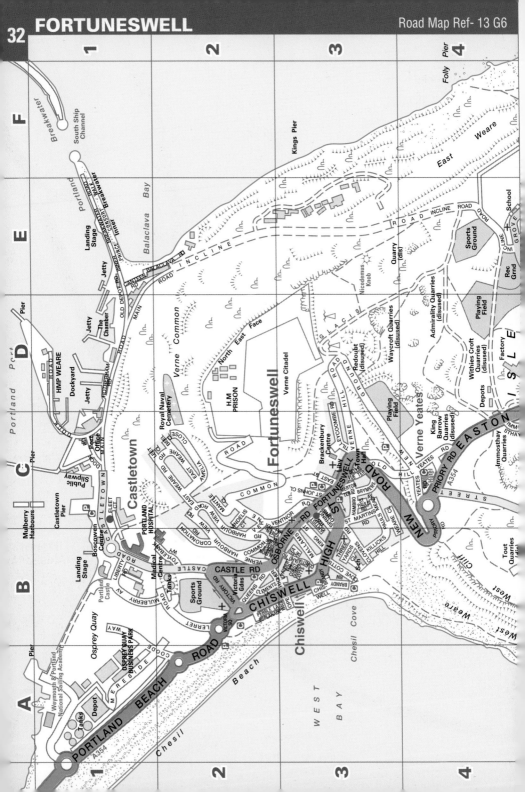

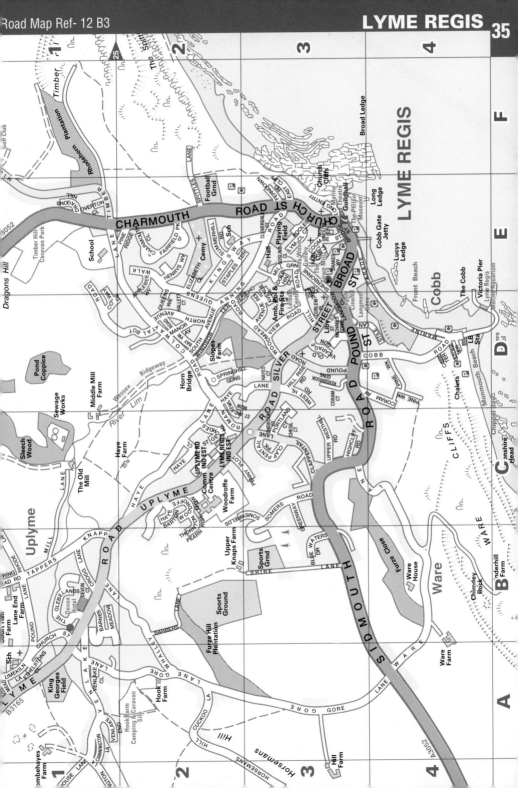

LYME REGIS

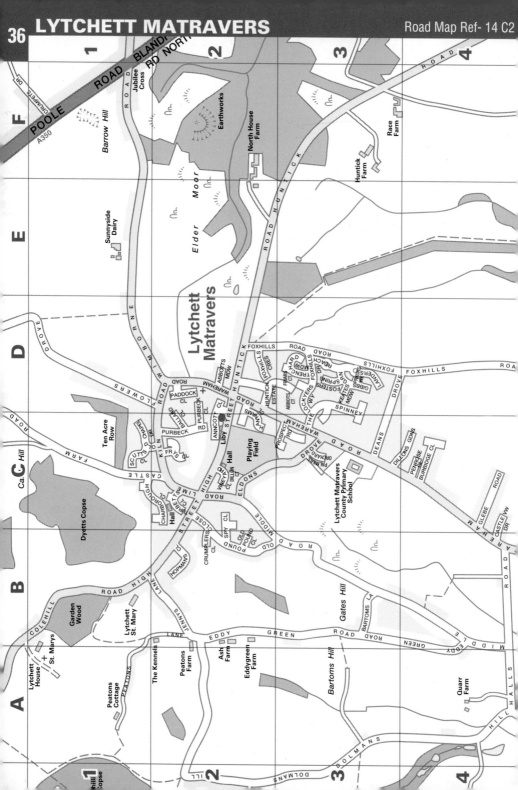

- Barrow Hill
- A350
- POOLE ROAD BLANDFORD
- Jubilee Cross
- RD NORTH
- Earthworks
- North House Farm
- Race Farm
- Huntick Farm
- ROAD HUNTICK
- Sunnyside Dairy
- Elder Moor
- Lytchett Matravers
- DROVE
- Ten Acre Row
- Dyetts Copse
- FARM ROAD
- Ca.C Hill
- WIMBOURNE ROAD
- FLOWERS
- CASTLE
- KILN
- CHAPEL
- SCUTS CL
- PADDOCK CL
- PURBECK
- BALLARD
- ANNCOT CL
- PURBECK RD
- HIGH STREET
- WAREHAM ROAD
- ABBOTS MDW
- FOXHILLS ESTATE
- FOXHILLS CRES
- FRIARS
- ORCHARD
- FOSTERS MDW
- GIBBS CL
- KEATES CL
- THE WY
- SPRING
- REACH
- SANDERS CL
- FOXHILLS
- FOXHILLS DROVE
- FOXHILLS ROAD
- SPINNEY
- DEANS
- DILLONS GDNS
- PENROSE
- BURBRIDGE CL
- CASTLE VW
- GLEBE ROAD
- ROAD
- Libby Hall
- Hall
- SWANS
- PROSPECT
- LOCKYERS DRIVE
- TRENCHARD
- PALMERS MDW
- DROVE
- Playing Field
- VINEY CL
- DILLIN CL
- ELDONS
- FR YS
- CL
- MIDDLE ROAD
- CLOSE
- SPY CL
- OLD POUND CL
- CRUMPLERS CL
- HOPMANS CL
- SCARBROUGH CL
- Hall
- LIME ST
- CHARBROUGH CL
- Lytchett Matravers County Primary School
- OLD POUND ROAD
- GATES Hill
- BARTOMS La
- Bartoms Hill
- Quarr Farm
- ROAD
- GREEN ROAD
- MIDDLE ROAD
- EDDY GREEN ROAD
- COLEHILL
- Garden Wood
- Lytchett St. Mary
- St. Marys
- Lytchett House
- St. Mary
- Peatons Cottage
- The Kennels
- Peatons Farm
- Ash Farm
- Eddygreen Farm
- EDDY GREEN
- PERIONS LANE
- JENNYS LANE
- LANE
- HIGH ROAD
- DOLMANS
- HILL HALLS
- Copse

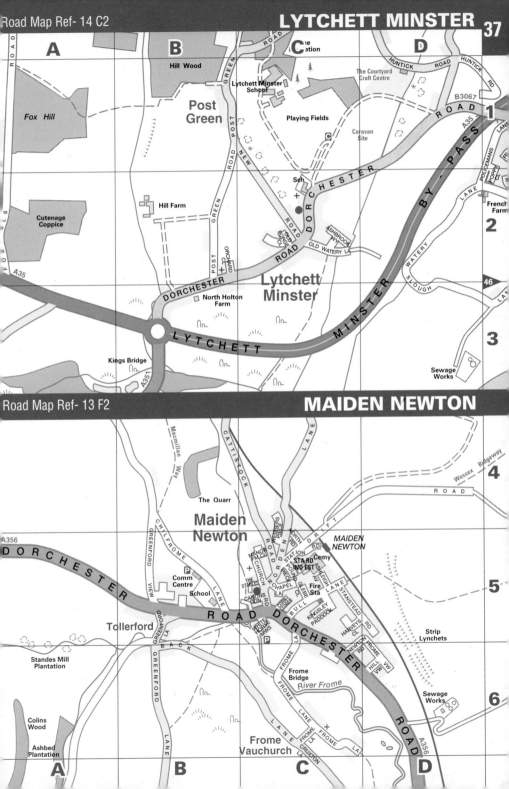

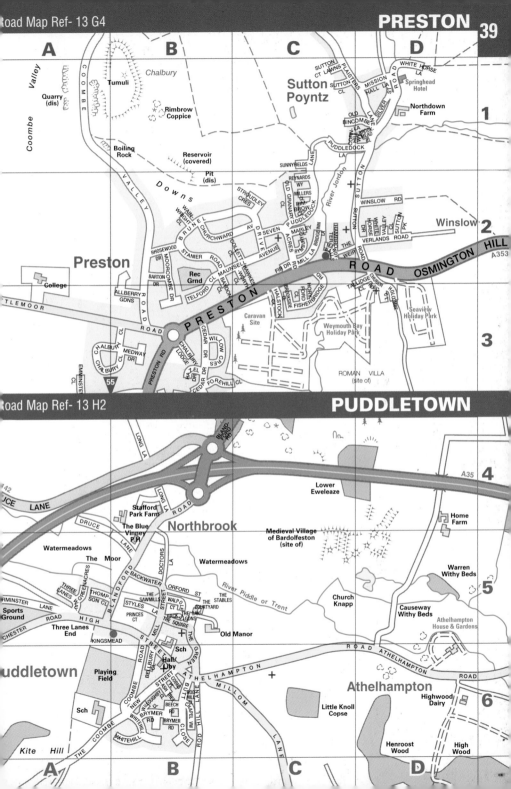

Sutton Poyntz

Preston

Winslow

College

WINSLOW RD

OSMINGTON HILL

A353

Caravan Site

Weymouth Bay Holiday Park

Seaview Holiday Park

ROMAN VILLA (site of)

Coombe Valley

Quarry (dis)

Tumuli

Chalbury

Rimbrow Coppice

Boiling Rock

Reservoir (covered)

Pit (dis)

Downs

VALLEY

55

A35

Lower Eweleaze

Home Farm

Stafford Park Farm

The Blue Vinney P.H.

Northbrook

Medieval Village of Bardolfeston (site of)

Warren Withy Beds

Watermeadows

The Moor

Watermeadows

River Piddle or Trent

Church Knapp

Causeway Withy Beds

Athelhampton House & Gardens

Sports Ground

Three Lanes End

KINGSMEAD

Old Manor

Puddletown

Playing Field

Sch

Sch

Hall/Lby

Athelhampton

Highwood Dairy

Little Knoll Copse

Henroost Wood

High Wood

Kite Hill

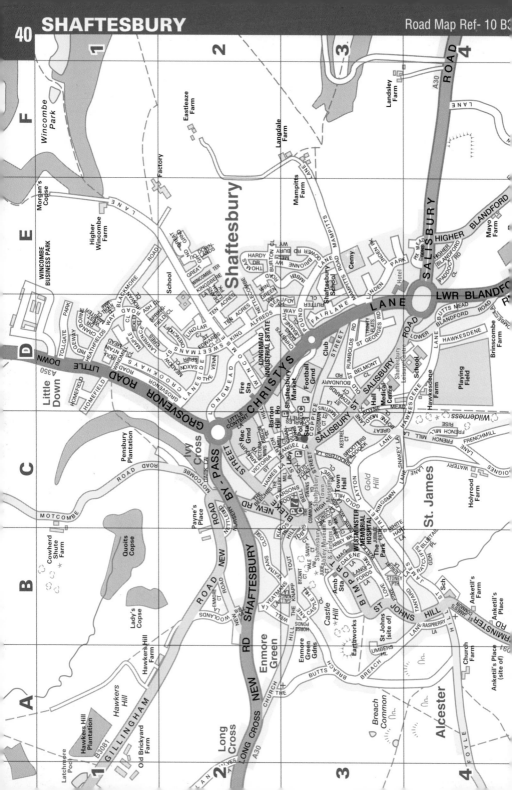

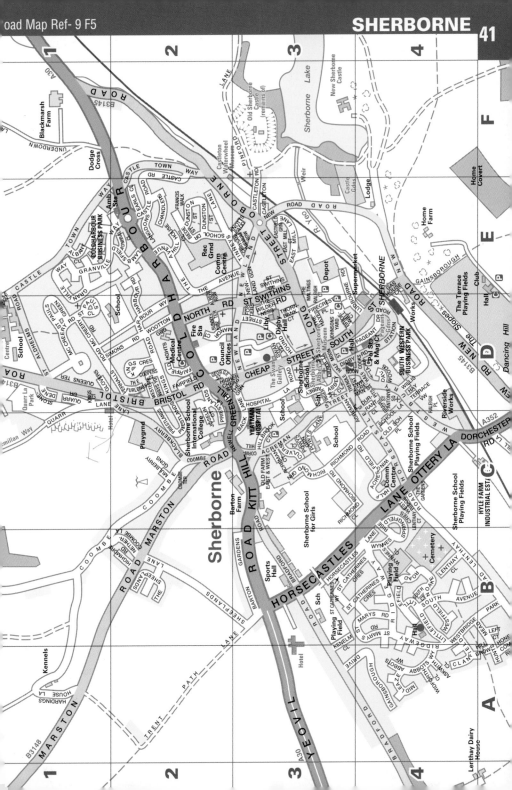

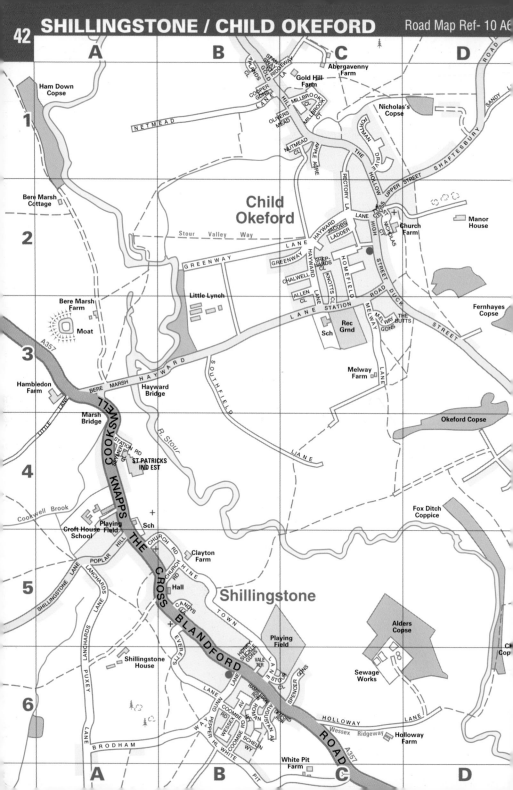

A   B   C   D

Ham Down Copse

Gold Hill Farm

Abergavenny Farm

Nicholas's Copse

NETMEAD

SPAR SKY GOLD RIDGEWAY
CL
UPLANDS CL
COPPER GDNS
LANE
GOLD HILL
OLIVERS MEAD
MILLBROOK CL
MILLBROOK CT
NUTMEAD CL
APPLE ACRE

1

Bere Marsh Cottage

Child Okeford

Stour Valley Way

GREENWAY

Little Lynch

GREENWAY

HAYWARD LANE

JACOBS LADDER

SHEP-HARDS CL

CHALWELL

KNOTS CL

ALLEN CL

HOMEFIELD

LANE

STATION

RECTORY LA.
LANE
HIGH STREET
CROSS ST
ST NICHOLAS CT
THE HOLLOW
PORTMAN DRIVE
UPPER STREET
SHAFTESBURY
SANDY L

Church Farm

Manor House

Fernhayes Copse

2

Bere Marsh Farm

Moat

A357

Rec Grnd

Sch

THE BUTTS
DYCK STREET
MELWAY
MELWAY GDNS

Melway Farm

Okeford Copse

3

Hambledon Farm

Marsh Bridge

HAYWARD

BERE MARSH

Hayward Bridge

SOUTHFIELD

R. Stour

LANE

LIANE

4

Cookwell Brook

Croft House School

Playing Field

STATION RD

SEYMER RD

ST PATRICKS IND EST

COOKSWELL

KNAPPS

Sch

Fox Ditch Coppice

5

POPLAR HILL

LANDSHARDS LANE

SHILLINGSTONE LANE

Clayton Farm

Hall

THE CROSS

CHURCH RD

CHURCH HINE RD

CANDYS

TOWN LANE

Shillingstone

Playing Field

Alders Copse

CH Cop

6

Shillingstone House

PUXEY LANE

BRODHAM

GUNN WAY

PEPPER HL

WHITE PIT LANE

COOMBE LANE

COOMBE RD

ROMAN WY

SCHELIN WY

HIDING SUICANE GDNS

VALE TER

STO

SPENCER GDNS

BLANDFORD

EVERETTS

AUGUSTAN AV

OXFORD ROW

A357

ROAD

HOLLOWAY LANE

Wessex Ridgeway

Holloway Farm

Sewage Works

White Pit Farm

A   B   C   D

A   B   C   D

Grays Farm

Wood Close

Home Farm

Sunnyridge Farm

A357

CHURCH HILL

DREWS LANE

St Mary

Church Covert

Sch

Mill

WOODMILL CL

1

Stalbridge Park

Manorial Earthworks

CHURCH

DUCK LANE

Liby

THE SIDINGS

STATION ROAD BUSINESS PARK

Stalbridge

HIGH STREET

MEADERS YARD

JARVIS

BACKMORE CRES

NEW RD

MAPLE ROW

GROVE

GOLD STREET

KNIGHTSTONE CT

GROVE LA

HILL

PC

The Old Corn Store

STALBRIDGE HILL

ROBINSONS HEIGHTS

MEADOW

YALE

BOYLE

DUR

RALEIGH WAY

YALE

WESSEX

PARK GRO

PARK RD

POND WK

BARROW LEA

Barrow Hill Farm

POUND

Hall

COPPERN WY

JARVIS CL

RALEIGH ROAD

LARKS MDW

SPRING FIELDS

THRIFT CL

THE HAWTHORNS

THE PADDOCKS

2

Rec Grnd

BARROW

WOOD

GROSVENOR RD

GROSVENOR RD

The Ring

WEST END MWS

RING ST

THORNHILL ROAD

BIBBERNE ROW

Basel Bridge

Harpitts

WATERLAKE

A357

Bibberne Bridge

3

ROAD

Wood Lane Farm

LANE

Bibberne Farm

Football Grnd

Sturminster Newton Leisure Centre

B3091

B3092

ROAD

School

Club Ho

NORTH FIELDS

CHURCH

CHICK

HOSEY

ELMSBURY

HONEYMEAD

CLOSE

4

Sturminster Newton

HONEYMEAD

Offices

School

SELWOOD CL

Rixon

CLOSE

ROAD

Colber Farm

oaks arm

River Stour

STALBRIDGE LANE

Stourcastle Centre

Sturminster Newton Museum

STOUR VIEW CL

QUARRY CL

BADGERS WAY

RABIN HILL

RIVERS MEAD

SHORTEDGE

ALDE

Playing Field

MANSTON ROAD

DENHALL CL

BUFFETTS

BUFFETTS RD

HANOVER CL

Fire Sta

THE GAVEL

PITTS ORCHARD

FILBRIDGE RISE

BUTTS POND IND EST

BUTT MWS

RICHMAR TRADING CENTRE

HAMBLEDON

ALDER

AVW

5

WHITE LANE CL

REDDLEMAN

DROVERS WAY

RIXON

COLES

CLOSE GREEN

BULL GROUND LANE

Pol Sta

Liby

BRINSLEY CL

BOLD MARKET

STATION ROAD

RIXON HILL

CHINNOCKS

FRIARS MOOR

ELM CLOSE

Sewage Works

6

Hall

THE ROW

GOUGHS CL

MKT PL

BRISTOL MKT CLOSE

BARNES CLOSE

PENNY LANE

FRIARS ARMS

CLOSE

FRIARS MOOR CT

GOTTS CORNER

Recreation Ground

RICKETTS LA

CROSS MWS

Mkt

ST MARKET

PENNY ST

CHURCH ST

GOTTS LA

HAM LA

Sch

DURRANT

BRIDGE

B3092

COACH RD

CHURCH LA

River Stour

LANE

A   B   C   D

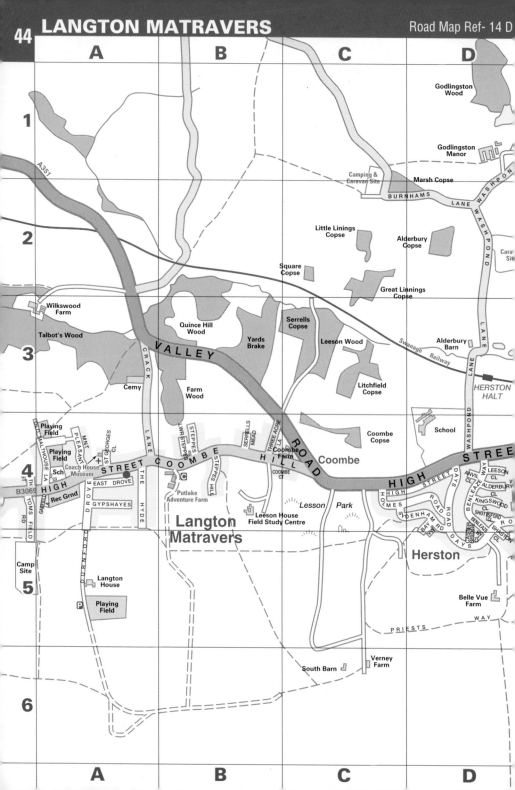

Godlingston Wood

Godlingston Manor

Camping & Caravan Site

Marsh Copse

BURNHAMS LANE WASHPOND

Cara Site

Little Linings Copse

Alderbury Copse

Square Copse

Great Linnings Copse

Wilkswood Farm

Quince Hill Wood

Serrells Copse

Talbot's Wood

Yards Brake

Leeson Wood

Alderbury Barn

VALLEY

CRACK LANE

Swanage Railway

HERSTON HALT

Cemy

Farm Wood

Litchfield Copse

WASHPOND LANE

Playing Field

Coombe Copse

School

Playing Field

MALTHOUSE LA

MNT PLEASANT

ST GEORGES CL

STEPPES

LWR STEPPES

SERRELLS MEAD

THREE ACRE LA

Coombe Farm

HIGH STREE

Sch

STREET COOMBE

Putlake Adventure Farm

COOMBE CT

Coombe

HIGH STREET DAYS RD

LEESON CL

ALDERBURY CL

ANVIL WAY

EAST DROVE

STEPPES HILL

COOMBE HILL ROAD

KINGSWOOD CL

HIGH ST

BENLEAZE

Rec Grnd

GYPSHAYES

B3069

TOMS FIELD RD

THE HYDE

HIGH ST

DROVE

QUEENS RD

Lesson Park

Leeson House Field Study Centre

Langton Matravers

Herston

HOLMES

SYDENHAM RD

DAYS ROAD

BAY

BENLEAZE

SHOTSFORD CL

SHASTON CL

Camp Site

Langton House

P

Playing Field

Belle Vue Farm

PRIESTS WAY

South Barn

Verney Farm

E   F   G   H

1

2

3

4

5

6

Works

Cemetery

Caravan Park

Swanage Farm

New Swanage

The Purbeck Centre

Cricket Grnd

Days Park

Rec Grnd

The Chatsworth Centre

Football Grnd

BALLARD

Cauldron Barn Farm

Cauldron Barn

Rec Grnd

School

BEACH GDNS

GAINSBOROUGH CT

Swanage Bay

VICTORIA AV IND EST

URBECK BSINESS ENTRE

VIVIAN PARK

BATTLEMEAD

HIGHCLIFFE RD

VICTORIA

GANNETTS PK

WALROND RD

RABLING LANE

WALROND ROAD

Sand Pit Field

Jetty

Playing Field

VICTORIA   AVENUE

King Georges Field

Swanage Railway

Cemy

Closed to Traffic May to Sept

SWANAGE

King Georges Field

SWANAGE

F.Sta

Tithe Barn Museum & Art Centre

The Mowlem Theatre

Swanage Heritage Centre

Swanage Pier

Youth Club

School

Liby

Quar Galler

Slipway

Convent MWS

Boat Yard

Amb Sta Sch

SWANAGE COMMUNITY HOSPITAL

Y.H.A.

PEVERIL POINT RD

Townsend Residential Centre

Caravan Park

Caravan Park

Hoburne Park

ATLANTIC RD

Townsend Nature Reserve

Playing Field

WEST DURLSTON LA

South Barn

Durlston Country Park

Durlston Bay

Durlston

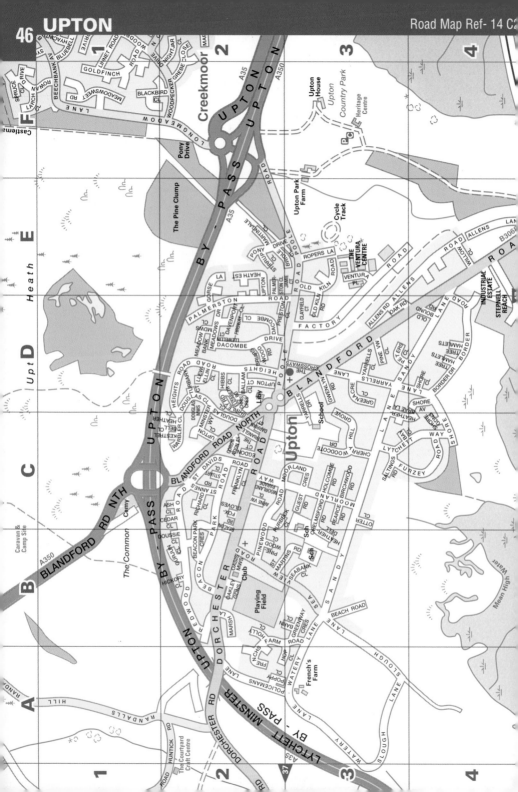

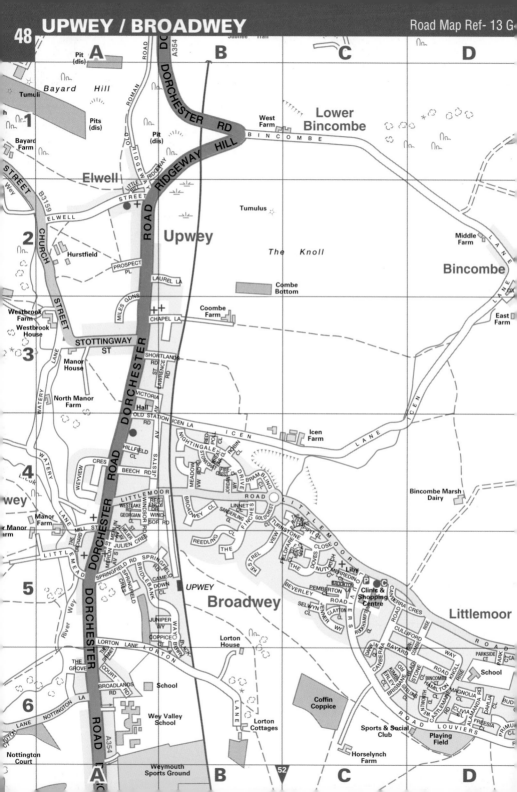

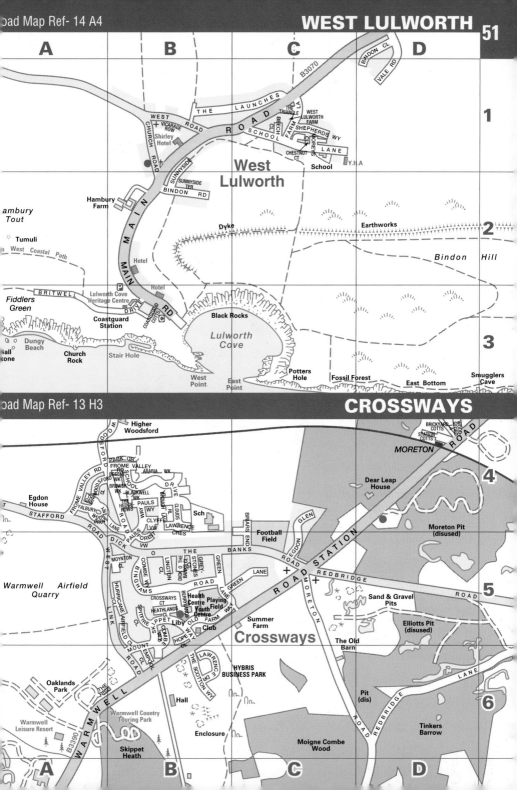

West Lulworth

A   B   C   D

1

B3070

BINDON CL
VALE RD

THE LAUNCHES
WEST ROAD
THE TRIANGLE
FARM LA
WEST LULWORTH FARM
SHEPHERDS WY
VICARAGE ROW
CHURCH ROAD
SHIRLEY Hotel
SCHOOL
BEECH
MOREYS
LANE
MOREYS
CHESTNUT CT
Y.H.A
School

SUNNYSIDE
SUNNYSIDE TER
BINDON RD

Hambury Farm

ambury Tout

2

Dyke   Earthworks

Tumuli

West Coastal Path

Bindon Hill

MAIN RD

Hotel

Hotel

BRITWELL
Lulworth Cove Heritage Centre
DRIVE
COASTGUARD COTTS
Fiddlers Green

Coastguard Station

Black Rocks

Lulworth Cove

3

Dungy Beach
Church Rock
Stair Hole

all one

Potters Hole

West Point
East Point

Fossil Forest
East Bottom
Smugglers Cave

Crossways

A   B   C   D

Higher Woodsford

BRICKYARD COTTS
STATION COTTS
MORETON
ROAD

PARK DR
FROME VALLEY RD
ARARIA WK
SCHOOL WK
BREWER WK
RESERVE WK
BLACKWELL
DRIVE
WRIGHT HL
CLOUDS HL
ST PAULS MS
ST PAULS AVN
CLYFFE
Sch
LAWRENCE CRES

4

Dear Leap House

Egdon House

STAFFORD
FROME VALLEY RD
YALBURY LANE
WOODS BROW
DICK O PAULS VW
ST PAULS VW

Moreton Pit (disused)

MOYNTON CL
COMBE WS
BINGHAM
LINGTON CL
THE GREY STONES
HILL O DICK
GREEN LANE
GREEN
BRIARS ENDS
Football Field
BANKS
GLEN
EGDON
ROAD STATION

5

Warmwell Airfield Quarry

HURRICANE CT
HEATHLANDS
CROSSWAYS CL
SPITFIRE XS
PPET CL
COMBE CL
BERRYMANS
Health Centre
Youth Centre
Liby
Playing Field
Club
FARM WAY
OLD FARM WAY
Summer Farm

REDBRIDGE ROAD

Sand & Gravel Pits

Elliotts Pit (disused)

LINK
HURRICANE AIRFIELD CL
MOUNT ROAD
ENPCOL
HOPE WAY
THE SPITFIRE WY
THE RISE
LAWRENCE WY

Crossways

The Old Barn

MORETON ROAD

6

Oaklands Park

WARMWELL ROAD
B3390

Hall

HYBRIS BUSINESS PARK

Pit (dis)

Warmwell Leisure Resort

Warmwell Country Touring Park

Skippet Heath

Enclosure

Moigne Combe Wood

REDBRIDGE ROAD
LANE

Tinkers Barrow

A   B   C   D

E   **F**   **G**   **H**

Field

Wyke Oliver Farm
39

Overcombe

Horse Lynch Plantation

Jordan   Hill

1

Wat
Ho
P

Jordon Hill
Roman Temple
(remains of)

New
Barn

COVEWAY

Bowle

BRACKENDOWN   AVENUE

PINE
MOOR
CL

MEW
MOOR
CL

OAK
MOOR
CL

SEA
MOOR
CL

MOORDOWN

EASTDOWN

HIGH
DOWN
AV

HAZELDOWN

Playground

RADLEY
CT

WILLOW
BROOK

Bo

2

Cliff

Furzy

SOUTHDOWN

AVENUE

KEAST
CT

HERON
CL

Overcombe
Court

Hide

BEACHDOWN

Lodmoor
Nature   Reserve
(RSPB)

Waste Centre

WAY

WALK

ESPLANADE

PRESTON   BEACH   ROAD

3

Miniature
Golf Course

Lodmoor
Country   Park

A353

Miniature
Railway

Sch

B
A
Y

GREENHILL

4

Sports
Ground

Aquarium &
Butterfly
Farm

Sea Life
Centre

Sk8
Park

Pirate
Adventure
Golf

Melcombe
Regis

P.H.

College

ROWLAND

ESPLANADE

W
E
Y
M
O
U
T
H

Greenhill
Gardens

eymouth
ollege

AVENUE

AVENUE

STANTON
CT

WEYMOUTH
COMMUNITY
HOSPITAL

Trimar
Hospice

5

B
A
Y

6

E   **F**   **G**   **H**

Jubilee Clock

55

WEYMOUTH

Kings Statue

KINGS ROUNDABOUT
R.S.P.B Office
Bus Sta
Jubilee Clock

WESTHAM R/BOUT
WESTHAM

Marina
Lbry
Shopping Centre

Seacat Ferry to Guernsey, Jersey & St. Malo

Pleasure Pier

Cineworld Cinema

Electric Palace

Pavilion Complex

Pier
Stone Pier

Courts
Offices
Harbour

Ferry
Commercial

The Mixen

Lakeside Superbowl

Deep-Sea Adventure

Nothe Fort

Superstore
Fire Stn
Offices

Town Bridge
Old Harbour

Nothe Gardens

Nothe Point

Barracks

CHAPELHAY

Tudor Ho
Mus

Brewers Quay

CEFAS H.Q.

Timewalk Museum

Newtons Cove

Rodwell

Depot

Rodwell Trail

PORTLAND BREAKWATER

Landing Stage

Landing Stage

Bincleaves Groyne

Landing Stage

Ledges

Western

Landing Stage
Castle Cove

Sandsfoot Castle (remains of)

West Moors

WEST MOORS PLANTATION

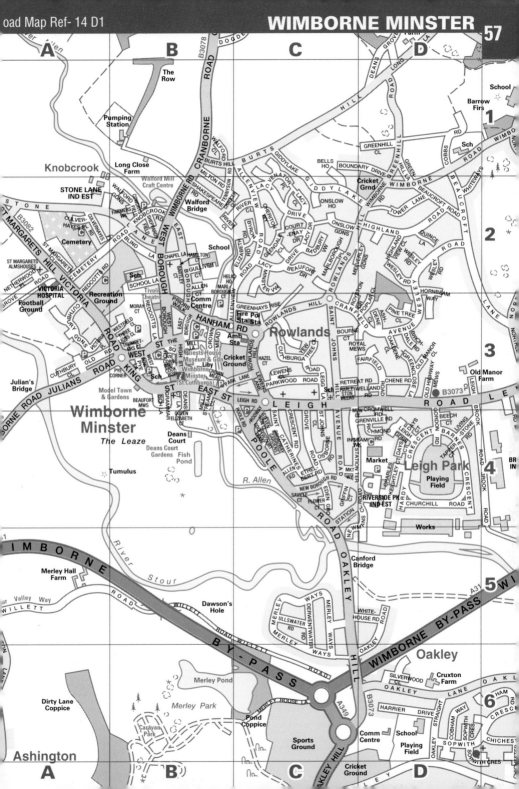

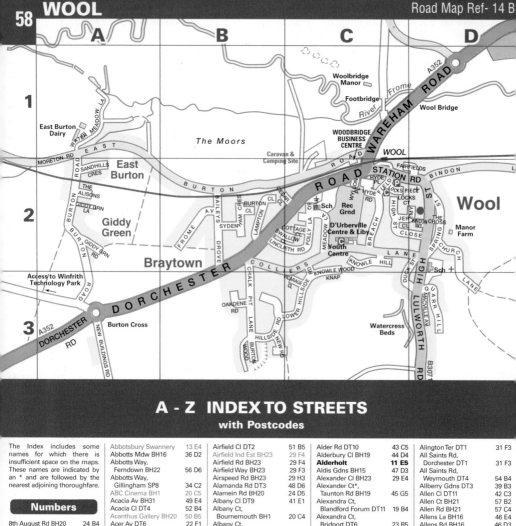

A - Z INDEX TO STREETS
with Postcodes

The Index includes some names for which there is insufficient space on the maps. These names are indicated by an * and are followed by the nearest adjoining thoroughfare.

Campion Gro BH23 29 F4
Canberra Cres DT3 48 C5
Canberra Rd DT3 48 C6
Candys La DT11 42 B5
Canford Rd BH15 38 C3
Cann **10 B4**
Cann Common **10 B4**
Cannington La DT7 35 A1
Canons Gdn DT2 37 C5
Canteen Rd DT5 32 E1
Canterbury Cl,
  Ferndown BH22 56 B6
Canterbury Cl,
  Weymouth DT4 54 B1
Capesthorne BH22
Capitol Cl DT1 30 D5
Capper Rd East BH20 24 C5
Capper Rd West BH20 24 B5
Capstone Gdns BH8 21 F2
Capstone Pl BH8 21 F2
Capstone Rd BH8 20 D1
Captains Cove BH15 47 D2
Caradon Pl BH31 49 A1
Carey Cl BH20 50 A4
Carisbrooke Cres BH15 47 C2
Carisbrooke DT4 52 B5
Carlton Rd BH1 21 E4
Carlton Rd North DT4 52 D5
Carlton Rd South DT4 52 D6
Carmen Cl BH15 47 D3
Carnarvon Rd BH1 21 G4
Caroline Av BH23 29 E5
Caroline Pl*, Park St DT4 55 F1
Carradale BH23 29 H3
Carrants Ct*,
  Cowlease BH19 45 F5
Carrick Cl DT1 31 G5
Carrington Cl DT4 54 D4
Carrion La BH20 50 C5
Carter Cl DT11 19 D3
Carters Av BH15 47 C1
Carters La BH15 38 B5
Cartref Cl BH31 49 C2
Carysfort Rd BH1 21 F3
Caseberry Ct DT1 30 B4
Cashmoor **10 D5**
Cassiobury Rd DT4 52 D6
Casterbridge Cl,
  Blandford Forum DT11 19 D2
Casterbridge Cl,
  Swanage BH19 44 D5
Casterbridge Rd DT1 31 H4
Casterbridge Trading Est
  DT1 31 F2
Casterbridge Way SP8 34 B1
Castle Cary
  & District Museum 9 G2
Castle Cl DT1 30 C4
Castle Farm Rd BH16 36 C2
Castle Hill Cl SP7 40 B3
Castle Hill Rd DT4 54 B5
Castle Neroche 8 A5
Castle Rd, Portland DT5 32 B2
Castle Rd,
  Sherbourne DT9 41 E2
Castle Sq DT6 23 C5
Castle St,
  Christchurch BH23 28 B4
Castle St, Poole BH15 38 B6
Castle Town Way DT9 41 D1
Castle View Dr BH16 36 B4
Castlemaine Rd DT3 48 D6
Castleman Ct BH22 56 A4
Castleman Smith Cl DT11 19 C2
Castleton DT9 41 E3
Castleton Rd DT9 41 E3
Castleton Waterwheel
  Museum DT9 41 F2
Castletown DT5 32 B1
Caswell Ct DT3 48 D6
Catalina Cl BH23 29 G4
Catalina Dr BH16 38 C6
Caters Pl DT1 31 E2
Catherines Ct*,
  St Catherines BH21 57 C4
Cattistock **13 E1**
Cattistock Rd DT2 37 B4
Cauldon Av BH19 45 G3
Cauldron Barn Rd BH19 45 F2
Cauldron Cres BH19 45 F2
Cauldron Mdws BH19 45 F3
Causeway Cl,
  Wareham BH20 50 B4
Causeway Cl,
  Weymouth DT4 52 A3

Causeway DT4 52 A3
Cavalcade of Costume
  Museum DT11 19 B4
Cavendish Hall BH1 20 C3
Cavendish Pl BH1 20 C3
Cavendish Rd BH1 20 C3
Caversham Cl BH15 47 D3
Cawdor Rd BH3 20 A1
Caxton Cl BH23 29 F3
Cecil Av BH8 21 E1
Cecil Cl BH21 27 D2
Cecil Rd,
  Bournemouth BH5 21 G4
Cecil Rd, Swanage BH19 45 F4
Cedar Cl, Poole BH16 46 C2
Cedar Cl,
  Wareham BH20 58 B2
Cedar Dr DT3 39 B3
Cedar Rd DT1 30 C3
Celandine Cl,
  Christchurch BH23 29 H2
Celandine Cl,
  Weymouth DT4 52 D4
Celtic Cres DT1 30 C5
Cemetery Rd,
  Gillingham SP8 34 C2,3
Cemetery Rd,
  Wimborne BH21 57 A2
Centenary Ho BH23 28 A3
Centenary Way BH1 21 G3
Central Av BH21 27 B1
Central Dr BH2 20 B3
Central Gardens 15 E3
Central Gdns BH2 20 A5
Central Pk DT11 18 C4
Centurion Rd DT11 18 C5
Cerne Abbas **13 G1**
Cerne Abbas Abbey
  & Well 13 G1
Cerne Av SP8 34 F4
Cerne Giant (NT) 13 G1
Chafeys Av DT4 52 A5
Chaffinch Chase SP8 34 E4
Chaffinch Cl DT3 48 C5
Chalbury Cl DT3 39 A3
Chalbury Common **10 D6**
Chalbury Lodge DT3 39 B3
Chaldon Herring **14 A4**
Chalk Pit Cl DT4 17 B3
Chalk Pit La BH20 58 B2
Chalky Rd DT2 17 A6
Challacombe St DT1 30 A3
Chalwell DT11 42 C2
Chamberlaine Rd DT4 54 B4
Champions DT8 16 B5
Chancery La DT6 22 C4
Chandler Cl DT3 52 D2
Chandlers DT9 41 E2
Channel View Rd DT5 33 C6
Channons Ct DT1 31 F3
Chant Cl BH23 28 D3
Chapel Cl BH21 27 B2
Chapel Gdns DT11 19 C4
Chapel La,
  Blandford Forum DT11 18 A3
Chapel La,
  Corfe Mullen BH21 27 A3
Chapel La,
  Dorchester DT2 37 C5
Chapel La, Poole BH15 38 B5
Chapel La,
  Swanage BH19 45 G4
Chapel La,
  Weymouth DT3 48 A3
Chapel La,
  Wimborne BH21 57 B2
Chapel Mews SP8 34 D2
Chapel Vw DT2 39 B6
Chapelhay St DT4 55 E2
Charberry Rise DT6 25 A5
Charborough Cl BH16 36 C2
Charborough Rd BH18 27 F4
Chard & District Museum 8 B6
Chards Mead Rd DT6 22 B3
Charles Garrett Cl SP7 40 C3
Charles Keightley Ct
  BH21 57 D4
Charles Rd, Bridport DT6 24 B2
Charles Rd,
  Christchurch BH23 29 F2
Charles Rd, Poole BH15 38 C3
Charles St,
  Blandford Forum DT11 19 C4
Charles St,
  Dorchester DT1 31 E3

Charles St,
  Weymouth DT4 52 D6
Charlestown **13 F5**
Charlmont Cross DT2 17 C6
Charlotte Cl,
  Christchurch BH23 29 G5
Charlotte Cl,
  Dorchester DT2 25 D3
Charlton Marshall **14 B1**
Charmile Ct DT3 52 C3
Charminster **13 G2**
Charminster La DT2 39 A5
Charminster Rd BH8 20 C2
Charmouth **12 B2**
Charmouth Cl DT7 35 E2
Charmouth Heritage
  Coast Centre DT6 25 B6
Charmouth Pl DT5 33 F5
Charmouth Rd DT7 35 E2
Charnwood Cl BH22 56 B4
Chartwell DT4 52 B4
Chase Cl BH31 49 F3
Chaseborough Sq DT1 30 B4
Chatsworth Rd BH8 21 E1
Chaucer Cl BH21 57 B2
Cheam Rd BH18 27 E4
Cheap St DT9 41 D3
Chedington **12 D1**
Chelmsford Rd BH16 46 B3
Chelmsford St DT1 30 C6
Chelwood Gate DT4 54 A1
Chene Rd BH21 57 D3
Cheriton Way BH21 57 C2
Cherry Grange BH8 21 E1
Cherry Hill Gro BH16 46 C3
Cherry Tree Ct DT11 18 A2
Cherry Tree DT6 22 B2
Cherry Way DT3 53 G2
Cherrybrook La DT1 30 A3
Cherryfields SP8 34 D1
Cherrytree La DT6 22 A1
Cheselbourne **13 H1**
Chesil Ct, Bridport DT6 24 B2
Chesil Ct,
  Lyme Regis DT7 35 C3
Chesil Ct,
  Weymouth DT4 54 A2
Chesil Pl DT1 31 E3
Chesil Vw DT4 54 B5
Chessel Av BH5 21 H3
Chester Cl DT1 31 G5
Chesterfield Ct BH1 21 E5
Chestnut Cl BH20 51 C1
Chestnut Gro DT11 19 A3
Chestnut Pl DT3 52 C3
Chestnut Rd DT6 23 C6
Chestnut Way,
  Dorchester DT1 30 C3
Chestnut Way,
  Gillingham SP8 34 B3
Chetnole **9 F6**
Chettell Way DT11 19 B6
Chettle **10 C5**
Chettle House 10 C5
Cheviot Ct BH23 29 E2
Cheviot Way BH31 49 C3
Chewton Glen 15 G2
Chichester Way BH23 29 G6
Chickerell **13 F4**
Chickerell Link Rd DT3 26 C3
Chickerell Rd,
  Charlestown DT3 26 B2
Chickerell Rd,
  Chickerell DT3 26 A1
Chickerell Rd,
  Weymouth DT4 54 A1
Chickerell Ter DT4 54 C2
Chideock **12 C3**
Chideock Ct DT7 35 C3
Chilcombe **13 E3**
Child Okeford **10 A5**
Chilcote Cl DT10 43 C5
Chilfrome La DT2 37 B4
Chiltern Cl*,
  Hunt Rd BH23 29 F2
Chiltern Dr BH31 49 C2
Chiltern Rd BH23 20 A6
Chine Cres BH2 20 A6
Chine Cres Rd BH2 20 A6
Chinnocks DT10 43 C5
Chiswell DT5 32 B2
Chivrick Ct DT10 43 C4
Cholderton Rare
  Breeds Farm Park 11 G1
Chorley Cl BH21 38 B1
Chris Cres BH16 46 C3

Christ Church Ct DT1 31 E3
Christchurch By-Pass
  BH23 28 B4
Christchurch Castle
  & Norman House BH23 28 B4
Christchurch Priory
  & St Michaels Loft Museum
  BH23 28 B5
Christchurch Rd BH1 21 E5
Christchurch Ski Centre 15 F1
Christchurch, **15 G3**
Christchurch,
  Bournemouth BH1 20 D5
Christmas Cl BH20 50 A5
Christopher Cres BH15 38 B3
Christys Gdns SP7 40 D3
Christys La DT9 40 C2
Chrysanthemum Cl*,
  Tinneys La DT9 41 E3
Chrysanthemum Row
  DT9 41 E3
Church Acre DT1 31 G3
Church Alley BH2 20 B5
Church Cl, Bridport DT6 22 F1
Church Cl,
  Dorchester DT1 31 F3
Church Cl,
  Swanage BH19 45 G4
Church Ct BH20 50 C6
Church Grn BH20 50 C6
Church Hill Ct BH31 49 B3
Church Hill,
  Shaftesbury SP7 40 C3
Church Hill,
  Sturminster Newton
  DT10 43 B1
Church Hill,
  Swanage BH19 45 F4
Church Hill,
  Verwood BH31 49 B2
Church Knapp DT4 54 C4
Church Knowle **14 C4**
Church La,
  Bere Regis BH20 17 C2
Church La,
  Blandford Forum DT11 19 B4
Church La,
  Christchurch BH23 28 B5
Church La,
  Dorchester DT2 25 C2
Church La,
  Shaftesbury SP7 40 C3
Church La,
  Sherbourne DT9 41 D3
Church La,
  Sturminster Newton
  DT10 43 B6
Church La,
  Wareham BH20 50 C6
Church La, Wool BH20 58 D2
Church Ope Rd DT5 33 E7
Church Rd,
  Maiden Newton DT2 37 C5
Church Rd,
  Pimperne DT11 18 A1
Church Rd,
  Shillingstone DT11 42 A5
Church Rd,
  Wareham BH20 51 B1
Church Rd,
  Weymouth DT3 39 D2
Church St,
  Beaminster DT8 16 B5
Church St, Bridport DT6 22 C4
Church St,
  Christchurch BH23 28 B4
Church St,
  Dorchester DT1 31 F3
Church St,
  Lyme Regis DT7 35 E3
Church St, Poole BH15 38 A6
Church St,
  Sturminster Newton
  DT10 43 B6
Church St, Uplyme DT7 35 A1
Church St,
  Wareham BH20 50 C6
Church St,
  Weymouth DT3 48 A2
Church St,
  Wimborne BH21 57 B3
Church Vw SP8 34 C3

Church Walk,
  Shaftesbury SP7 40 C3
Church Walk,
  Stalbridge DT10 43 B1
Church Walk,
  Sturminster Newton
  DT10 43 C6
Churchfield BH31 49 B2
Churchfield Cres BH15 38 D3
Churchfield Ct BH15 38 D4
Churchfield Rd BH15 38 D4
Churchill Cl,
  Fordingbridge SP6 16 A2
Churchill Cl,
  Weymouth DT4 54 B5
Churchill Cl BH1 21 G3
Churchill Gdns DT4 54 D4
Churchill Rd,
  Blandford Forum DT11 19 B3
Churchill Rd,
  Bournemouth BH1 21 G3
Churchill Rd,
  Wareham BH20 24 A4
Churchill Rd,
  Wimborne BH21 57 D4
Churchward Av DT3 39 B2
Churchwood Ct*,
  St Michaels Rd BH2 50 B6
Cineworld Cinema DT4 55 F2
Cinnamon La BH15 38 A6
Clanfield DT9 41 A4
Clapgate **14 D1**
Clappental La DT7 35 C3
Clappental Pk DT7 35 C3
Clare Av DT4 54 C2
Claremont Av SP8 34 C2
Claremont Gdns DT6 22 D2
Claremont Rd DT6 22 D2
Clarence Cl DT5 33 C6
Clarence Pl BH23 28 A2
Clarence Rd,
  Dorchester DT1 30 D5
Clarence Rd,
  Portland DT5 33 C6
Clarence Rd,
  Weymouth DT4 54 A3
Clarendon Av DT3 52 C1
Clarendon Cl,
  Broadstone BH18 27 F4
Clarendon Cl,
  Gillingham SP8 34 A3
Clarendon Rd,
  Broadstone BH18 27 E4
Clarendon Rd,
  Christchurch BH23 28 A3
Clarks Village 8 D1
Claudius Cl DT1 30 C6
Clay La DT8 16 A5
Clayfield Cl BH16 46 D3
Claylake Dr BH31 49 D3
Clayton Cl DT3 48 C5
Clematis Cl BH23 29 H2
Clements La DT5 32 B2
Cleveland Av DT3 52 D3
Cleveland Gdns BH1 21 F3
Cleveland Rd BH1 21 F2
Cleves Cl DT4 54 D5
Cliff Av BH19 45 G2
Cliff Dr BH23 29 H4
Cliff Pl*,
  Marshall Row BH19 45 G4
Cliff Rd DT6 24 B3
Clifford Ct SP8 34 B3
Clifton Cl BH19 45 G2
Clifton Ct BH5 21 H3
Clifton Pl*,
  Gloucester Mews DT4 55 F1
Clifton Rd BH19 45 G2
Clive Ter DT4 54 D1
Clivia Cl DT3 48 D6
Clouds Hill (NT) 14 A3
Clouds Hill DT2 51 B4
Clovens Rd DT5 32 B3
Clover Cl BH23 29 H2
Cloverdale Ct DT7 35 E3
Cloverfields SP8 34 C1
Clump Fm Ind Est DT11 19 B2
Cluny Cres BH19 45 G5
Clyffe Vw DT2 51 B4
Coach House Museum
  BH19 44 A4
Coach House Pl BH1 20 D3
Coach Rd DT10 43 B6
Coastguard Cotts,
  Portland DT5 32 B3

Coastguard Cotts, Wareham BH20 51 B3
Coastguard Rd DT5 32 B3
Coastguard Way BH23 29 E6
Cobb Rd DT7 35 D3
Cobb Ter DT7 35 D4
Cobbs La BH15 38 D1
Cobbs Pl DT2 39 B6
Cobbs Rd BH21 57 D1
Cobham Dr DT4 54 B1
Cobham Rd DT11 19 C2
Cobham Way BH21 57 D6
Coblers La BH19 45 F5
Coburg Ct DT1 30 D4
Coburg Pl*, St Thomas St DT4 55 F1
Coburg Rd DT1 30 C4
Cocklands DT2 25 C3
Cockles La DT4 54 A5
Cockroad La DT8 16 A4
Colborne Cl BH15 38 C6
Colchester Way DT4 54 B1
Coldharbour Bsns Pk DT9 41 E1
Coldharbour, Gillingham SP8 34 B2
Coldharbour, Sherbourne DT9 41 D2
Colehill 14 D1
Colehill Rd BH16 36 B1
Coleridge Grn BH23 29 F3
Coles Av BH15 47 D4
Coles Cl DT10 43 C5
Coles Gdns BH15 47 D3
Colin Cl BH21 27 C3
College Cl DT3 48 D2
College La DT4 53 E5
College Rd DT11 18 C4
Collett Cl DT3 39 B2
Colletts Cl BH20 26 C6
Colliers La BH20 58 B2
Collingwood Cl DT11 18 A2
Collingwood Rd BH21 56 B1
Collins La DT4 54 B5
Colliton St DT1 31 E3
Colliton Walk DT1 31 E2
Colman Ct BH1 21 F5
Cologne Rd BH20 24 C5
Columbine Cl BH23 29 H1
Colway Cl DT7 35 D1
Colway La DT7 35 D2
Combe Way DT2 51 B5
Comet Cl DT4 54 B3
Comet Way BH23 29 G4
Commercial Rd, Bournemouth BH2 20 A5
Commercial Rd, Swanage BH19 45 G4
Commercial Rd, Weymouth DT4 55 E1
Common La, Bridport DT6 22 C4
Common Mead Av SP8 34 C3
Common Mead La SP8 34 A4
Compton Abbas 10 B4
Compton Acres 14 D3
Compton Cl BH31 49 C2
Compton Cres BH22 56 D5
Compton Valence 13 F2
Conches Ct DT6 50 B5
Concorde Cl DT4 54 B3
Condor Cl BH21 56 D1
Coneygar Cl DT6 22 C2
Coneygar La DT6 22 D2
Coneygar Rd DT6 22 C2
Conifer Way DT4 52 B4
Coniston Cl BH31 49 B3
Coniston Cres DT3 52 C3
Connaught Gdns DT4 54 D3
Connaught Rd DT4 54 D4
Connell Rd BH15 38 B2
Conniger La BH20 50 C6
Convent Mews BH19 45 G4
Conway Dr DT2 17 B6
Conway Walk DT1 31 G5
Coode Way DT5 32 A2
Cook Row BH21 57 B3
Cooks La DT9 41 D4
Cooks Mead DT7 35 A1
Cookswell DT11 42 A4
Coombe Av DT4 54 B3
Coombe Ct BH19 44 B4
Coombe DT9 41 B1

Coombe Hill BH19 44 A4
Coombe Keynes 14 B4
Coombe Rd, Blandford Forum DT11 42 B6
Coombe Rd, Dorchester DT2 39 B6
Coombe St DT7 35 E3
Coombe Ter DT9 41 C2
Coombe Valley Rd DT3 39 A1
Cooper Ct*, Fulbrooks La DT6 22 B3
Cooper Gdns DT11 42 B1
Coopercourt Leaze BH21 57 C4
Coopers Cl BH20 50 B5
Coopers Ct DT9 41 D2
Coopers Dr DT6 23 D6
Coopers La BH31 49 B1
Coppers Way DT10 43 C2
Coppers Cl SP6 16 C2
Coppice Ct DT3 48 A5
Coppice St SP7 40 C3
Copse Rd BH31 49 C2
Coram Av DT7 35 D4
Coram Ct DT7 35 D3
Corbin Way DT6 22 E1
Cordery Gdns SP8 34 C1
Cordova Gdns DT9 22 D3
Corfe Castle 14 C4
Corfe Castle & Museum (NT) BH20 26 B4
Corfe Lodge Rd BH21 27 B4
Corfe Mews BH15 38 C3
Corfe Mullen 14 C2
Corfe Rd DT3 52 B2
Corfe View Rd BH21 27 B3
Corn Market BH21 57 B3
Cornflower Dr BH23 29 H1
Cornhill Way DT3 39 C1
Cornhill, Dorchester DT1 31 E3
Cornhill, Sherbourne DT9 41 C3
Cornstores DT2 37 C5
Cornwall Cl DT4 54 C1
Cornwall Rd, Dorchester DT1 31 E3
Cornwall Rd, Swanage BH19 45 G4
Coronation Av BH16 46 C2
Coronation Cl BH31 49 B1
Coronation Cres DT3 52 C3
Coronation Rd, Bridport DT6 22 B4
Coronation Rd, Gillingham SP8 34 C2
Coronation Rd, Portland DT5 32 B2
Coronation Rd, Verwood BH31 49 C1
Coronation Rd, Weymouth DT3 52 C4
Corporation Rd, Bournemouth BH1 21 E3
Corporation Rd, Weymouth DT4 54 C1
Corporation Rd DT4 52 B6
Corscombe 8 D6
Corscombe Cl DT4 55 E1
Cotlands Rd BH1 20 D4
Cotswold Cl BH31 49 C3
Cotswold Cl BH23 29 F2
Cottage Cl BH20 58 B2
Cotton Cl BH18 27 E3
Counter Cl DT11 19 D3
Court Barton DT5 33 B6
Court Cl, Christchurch BH23 29 E4
Court Hill BH19 45 F4
Court Orchard Rd DT6 22 B2
Court Rd, Swanage BH19 45 F4
Court Rd, Weymouth DT3 48 A6
Courtauld Dr DT4 54 C4
Courtenay Cl BH20 50 C3
Courtenay Dr BH21 57 C2
Courtlands Rd DT5 33 B7
Courtleigh Manor BH1 21 F4
Courtney Pl BH21 27 B3
Cove Cotts DT5 32 B3
Cove Pass*, Cove Row DT4 55 F2
Cove Pl*, Cove Row DT4 55 F2
Cove Row DT4 55 F2
Cove St*, Cove Row DT4 55 F2
Coventry Cl BH21 27 A4

Coveside DT3 53 G2
Cow Dro BH20 17 C1
Cow La, Swanage BH19 45 E4
Cow La, Wareham BH20 50 B6
Cowdrys Fld BH21 57 B2
Cowgrove Rd BH21 57 A3
Cowlease BH19 45 F5
Cowleaze Rd DT2 17 B6
Cowley Cl DT1 30 C3
Crabton Close Rd BH5 21 H4
Crack La BH19 44 A3
Cranborne 11 E5
Cranborne Dr SP7 40 D1
Cranborne Garden 10 D5
Cranborne Rd, Bournemouth BH2 20 B6
Cranborne Rd, Swanage BH19 45 G4
Cranborne Rd, Wimborne BH21 57 B1
Crane Cl BH31 49 B2
Crane Dr BH31 49 B2
Cranes Mews BH15 38 C4
Cranesmoor Cl BH20 24 A5
Cranfield Av BH21 57 C3
Cranford Av DT4 53 E5
Crawford Down Rd DT11 18 C6
Creech Way DT3 52 B2
Creedy Dr BH23 28 A5
Creedy Path BH23 28 B4
Crescent Rd, Bournemouth BH2 20 A5
Crescent Rd, Verwood BH31 49 D2
Crescent Rd, Wimborne BH21 57 C4
Crescent St DT4 55 F1
Cresscombe Cl SP8 34 C1
Crewkerne & District Museum 8 D6
Cricket Cl BH23 29 F5
Cricket St Thomas Wildlife Park 8 C6
Cringle Av BH6 28 A6
Crispins Cl DT4 54 B4
Crock La DT6 23 D5
Croft Cl BH21 27 B1
Croft Rd, Christchurch BH23 29 F3
Croft Rd, Portland DT5 33 A6
Crogg La DT7 35 B1
Cromer Rd BH8 21 F1
Cromwell Rd, Dorchester DT1 31 E4
Cromwell Rd, Weymouth DT4 54 D1
Cromwell Rd, Wimborne BH21 57 D4
Crookhays SP7 40 D2
Cross Rd DT4 54 D4
Crosstree Cl DT2 17 B6
Crossway DT11 18 C4
Crossways 13 H3
Crossways Cl DT4 51 B5
Crouch Hill BH23 28 D3
Crow Hill Ct BH15 38 D3
Crown Farm Ter DT5 33 D5
Crown Mead BH21 57 B3
Crumpets Dr BH16 36 F1
Crumplers Cl BH16 36 B2
Cruxton La DT2 37 C6
Cuckoo Cl BH20 50 C5
Cuckoo La DT7 35 A2
Culford CP BH8 20 C2
Culliford Rd North DT1 31 F4
Culliford Rd South DT1 31 F4
Culliford Way DT3 48 C5
Culverhayes Cl BH21 57 A2
Culverhayes DT8 16 A5
Culverhayes Pl BH21 57 A2
Culverhayes Rd BH21 57 A2
Culvers Cl DT3 41 C3
Cumberland Dr DT4 54 A1
Cumnor Rd*, Lorne Pk Rd BH1 20 C5
Cunningham Cl, Christchurch BH23 29 F4
Cunningham Cl, Wareham BH20 24 C5
Cunningham Cl, Weymouth DT4 54 D1
Cunnington Cl DT1 30 D6
Curlew Cl DT3 26 B2
Curlew Pl DT7 35 D3
Curlew Rd BH23 29 F4

Curlieu Rd BH15 38 C1
Curzon Rd BH1 21 F2
Custom Ho Quay*, Maiden St DT4 55 F2
Cuthburga Rd BH21 57 C3
Cuthbury Cl BH21 57 A3
Cuthbury Gdns BH21 57 A3
Cutsome Cl DT1 31 F5
Cypress Way SP8 34 C2
Cyril Rd BH8 21 E2
Cyril Wood Ct BH20 17 C2

D

Dacombe Cl BH16 46 D2
Dacombe Dr BH16 46 D2
Daggons Rd SP6 16 A2
Dagmar Rd DT1 30 D4
Dahlia Cl DT3 48 D6
Dahlia Ct BH15 38 D1
Dairy Cl, Christchurch BH23 28 D4
Dairy Cl, Wimborne BH21 57 A4
Dairy Fld DT11 19 D2
Daisy Cl BH15 38 C1
Dakota Cl BH23 29 G4
Dale Av DT4 52 D4
Dale Cl BH31 38 D1
Daler Ct BH20 50 C5
Dalkeith Rd BH21 57 C4
Dalkeith La*, Richmond Gdns BH1 20 B4
Dalwoods DT9 41 D4
Damers Ct DT1 30 D3
Damers Rd DT1 30 C3
Damory Court St DT11 19 C4
Damory Ct DT11 19 C4
D'Amory Mews DT11 19 C3
Damory St DT11 19 B4
Daniel Dr BH20 50 B3
Daniel Gdns*, Skinner St BH15 38 B6
Darby La DT6 24 B2
Darbys Cl BH15 38 C1
Darbys La BH15 38 C1
Darcy Ct DT11 19 B3
Dark La, Bridport DT6 23 B3
Dark La, Shaftesbury SP7 40 C2
Dark La, Wareham BH20 17 A1
Darkie La BH19 45 F1
Darrian Ct BH16 46 C2
Darwin Cl DT3 48 C6
Dashwood Cl DT10 43 C4
Davenant Cl SP8 34 B3
Davenport Dr BH16 46 D2
Davenport Ct DT4 55 E1
David Way BH15 47 C3
Davis Gdns DT11 19 C2
Dawkins Rd BH15 47 C2
Dawlish Cres DT4 54 D5
Days Ct BH21 57 D4
Days Rd BH19 44 D4
De Legh Gro DT6 22 A3
De Lisle Rd BH3 20 B1
De Moulham Rd BH19 45 G2
Dean 10 D5
Dean Cl BH15 47 D2
Dean Park Cres BH1 20 C4
Dean Park Gate BH2 20 B4
Dean Park Rd BH1 20 C4
Deane Av SP8 34 B3
Deanland 10 C4
Deans Court Gardens BH21 57 B4
Deans Court La BH21 57 B3
Deans Dro BH16 36 C3
Deans Gro BH21 57 D1
Deansleigh Pk SP7 40 D2
Dear Hay La BH15 38 B5
Dee Way BH15 38 A6
Deep Sea Adventure DT4 55 F2
Deer Park Rd DT11 19 B4
Dehavilland Way BH23 29 F5
Delapre Gdns DT6 22 D3
Delft Mews*, Scotts Hill La BH23 28 D4
Delhi La DT5 33 D6
Delilah Rd BH15 47 C3
Dell Cl BH18 27 D4
Delta Cl BH23 29 G3
Denby Rd BH15 38 C4
Denewood Copse BH22 56 A3

Denewood Rd BH22 56 A3
Denhall Cl DT10 43 B5
Denmark La BH15 38 C4
Denmark Rd BH15 38 C4
Dennis Rd, Weymouth DT4 54 C2
Dennis Rd, Wimborne BH21 27 C3
Dennistoun Av BH23 29 E3
Derby Rd BH1 21 E4
Derby St DT4 52 D6
Derwent Rd DT4 54 C6
Derwentwater Rd BH21 57 C5
Devenish Cl DT4 55 F4
Devenish Gdns DT4 55 E3
Devenish Warren DT4 55 F4
Deverel Cl BH23 28 A2
Devon Ct DT7 35 B1
Devon Rd, Poole BH15 38 D2
Devon Rd, Weymouth DT4 52 B6
Devonedge La DT6 25 C4
Deweys Way SP8 34 C2
Dewlands Pk BH31 49 A2
Dewlands Rd BH31 49 A1
Dewlands Way BH31 49 A1
Dewlish 14 A2
Dewsall Pl*, Harewood Rd DT1 30 B3
Diana Cl DT1 30 D5
Diana Way BH21 27 D1
Dick O The Banks Cl DT2 51 B5
Dick O The Banks Rd DT2 51 B5
Digby Cl DT1 30 D4
Digby Rd DT9 41 D3
Diggory Cr DT1 31 F5
Diggory Cres DT1 31 F5
Dillington House 8 B5
Dillon Cl BH16 36 C2
Dillons Gdns BH16 36 C3
Diments Gdns DT6 22 B2
Diments Sq DT6 22 B2
Dingley Rd BH15 38 C1
Dinham Walk DT1 30 B3
Dinosaur Museum DT1 31 F3
Dinosaurland 12 B3
Diprose Rd BH21 27 C1
Discovery 13 G5
Disraeli Rd BH23 28 D4
Dock Rd DT5 32 C1
Doctors La DT2 39 B5
Dodhams Farm Cl DT6 22 C1
Dodhams La DT6 22 D1
Does La BH31 49 A2
Dollins La BH20 50 B5
Dolphin Centre BH15 38 B5
Dolphin Cl DT7 35 E3
Dolphin Ct BH19 45 G3
Dolphin La SP8 34 C1
Dolphin Swimming Pool BH15 38 C5
Doncaster Rd DT4 54 C6
Donkey La, Bridport DT6 22 B2
Donkey La, Burton Bradstock DT6 24 B2
Donnington Dr BH23 29 H3
Donoughmore Rd BH1 21 G4
Dorchester 13 G3
Dorchester Arts Centre DT1 31 E2
Dorchester By-Pass DT1 30 A4
Dorchester Gdns BH15 38 D3
Dorchester Hill DT11 19 A6
Dorchester Mansions BH1 21 F5
Dorchester Rd, Bridport DT6 22 F3
Dorchester Rd, Broadwey DT3 48 A5
Dorchester Rd, Lytchett Minster BH16 37 B3
Dorchester Rd, Maiden Newton DT2 37 A5
Dorchester Rd, Poole BH15 38 C1
Dorchester Rd, Puddletown DT2 39 A5
Dorchester Rd, Sherbourne DT9 41 C4
Dorchester Rd, Upwey DT3 48 B1
Dorchester Rd, Wareham BH20 58 A3
Dorchester Rd, Weymouth DT3 52 B1

Limekiln La DT7 35 A1
Linclieth Rd BH20 58 B2
Lincoln Av BH1 21 F2
Lincoln Rd DT4 54 B2
Linden Av DT1 31 F3
Linden Pk SP7 40 D3
Linden Rd BH19 45 F4
Lindens Cl DT4 52 C4
Lindlar Cl SP7 40 D2
Lineside BH23 28 C2
Lington Cl DT2 51 B5
Lingwood Av BH23 29 E4
Link Rise BH21 27 C2
Links Est DT4 26 D3
Links Rd DT4 52 B6
Linnet Cl DT3 48 B4
Linnet Rd BH11 46 F1
Linsay Rd BH20 24 B6
Linthorpe Rd BH15 38 D3
Linwood Rd BH9 20 D1
Lions Cl BH15 38 C3
Liscombe Cl DT1 30 C3
Little Britain DT1 31 G3
Little Content La SP7 40 D1
Little Dewlands BH31 49 A2
Little Down SP7 40 D1
Little Forest Rd BH4 20 A2
Little Hill DT3 48 A2
Little La DT11 42 A4
Littlebredy 13 E3
Littledown Av BH7 21 G1
Littledown Dr BH7 21 G1
Littlefield DT9 41 B4
Littlemead,
 Dorchester DT2 17 B6
Littlemead,
 Weymouth DT3 48 A5
Littlemoor Rd,
 Broadwey DT3 48 A4
Littlemoor Rd,
 Preston DT3 39 A3
Littlesea Ind Est DT4 54 A2
Littletowns DT11 19 C2
Littleview Rd DT4 54 B3
Litton Cheney 13 E3
Liverpool Rd DT4 54 B3
Livingstone Rd,
 Christchurch BH23 28 D4
Livingstone Rd,
 Wimborne BH21 57 D4
Llewellin Cl BH16 46 D2
Llewellin Cl BH16 46 D2
Locarno Rd BH19 45 F4
Lockeridge Cl DT11 19 B3
Locks Cl BH20 58 C2
Locks Piece BH20 58 C2
Lockwood Ter SP8 34 F4
Lockyers Way BH16 36 D3
Lodbourne Gdns SP8 34 C2
Lodbourne Green Par*,
 Lodbourne Grn SP8 34 D2
Lodbourne Grn SP8 34 D2
Lodbourne Ter SP8 34 C2
Lodden Vw SP8 34 E4
Loders 12 D2
Lodge La DT6 22 A3
Lodge Way DT4 54 C4
Lodmoor Av DT3 52 D3
Lodmoor Country Park
 DT4 53 E4
Lodmoor Nature Reserve
 (RSPB) DT3 53 F3
Lombardy Cl BH31 49 E3
Lomond Dr DT4 54 C4
London Cl DT1 31 G3
London Rd DT1 31 F3
Long Acre DT5 33 D6
Long Bredy 13 F3
Long Cl DT10 43 C4
Long Crichel 10 C6
Long Entry DT7 35 E3
Long La, Bridport DT6 23 D6
Long La, Dorchester DT2 39 B4
Long La,
 Wimborne BH21 57 D1
Long St SP7 41 D3
Longburton 9 G5
Longcroft Rd DT4 54 D1
Longfield Rd DT4 55 E3
Longfleet Rd BH15 38 C4
Longham 15 E2
Longhayes Av DT6 23 C8
Longmead Ind Est SP7 40 D2
Longmead SP7 40 C2
Longmeadow La BH17 46 F2

Longmoor St DT1 30 B4
Long's Ct DT6 22 B3
Longs La DT6 22 D3
Longstone Cl DT5 33 B8
Lonsdale Rd BH3 20 B1
Lorne Park Rd BH1 20 C5
Lorne Rd DT1 30 D4
Lornton Walk DT1 31 F5
Lorton La DT3 48 A5
Loughwood
 Meeting House (NT) 12 A1
Louise Rd DT1 30 D4
Louviers Rd DT3 48 C5
Love La,
 Shaftesbury SP7 40 B3
Love La, Weymouth DT4 55 E3
Lower Acreman St DT9 41 D3
Lower Blakemore Rd*,
 Woodlands Cres DT1 30 A3
Lower Blandford Rd,
 Broadstone BH18 27 F4
Lower Blandford Rd,
 Shaftesbury SP7 40 D4
Lower Central Gardens 15 E3
Lower Central Gdns BH1 20 C5
Lower Cranesmoor BH20 24 A5
Lower Golf Links Rd
 BH18 27 F3
Lower Hillside Rd BH20 58 B3
Lower Kingcombe 13 E1
Lower Putton La DT3 26 C1
Lower Rd DT10 43 C2
Lower St Alban St DT4 55 E2
Lower School La DT11 19 B6
Lower Sea La DT6 25 C6
Lower Severalls
 Garden & Nursery 8 D5
Lower Steppes BH19 44 B4
Lower Townsend DT6 24 C1
Lower Walditch La DT6 22 E4
Lower Way DT3 26 B1
Lowther Gdns BH8 21 E3
Lowther Rd BH8 20 D2
Lubbecke Way DT1 31 G3
Lucas Rd BH15 38 A6
Lucetta La DT1 31 F4
Ludbourne Rd DT9 41 D4
Ludlow Rd DT4 54 B2
Lugger Cl DT3 26 A1
Lulworth Av BH15 47 D4
Lulworth Castle 14 B4
Lulworth Cl BH15 47 D4
Lulworth Cove
 Heritage Centre BH20 51 A3
Lulworth Cres BH15 47 D4
Lulworth Rd BH20 58 D3
Lush Path*,
 Dunston St DT9 41 E2
Luton Down Rd DT11 18 C6
Lydfords La SP8 34 A3
Lydgate St DT1 30 A3
Lydlinch 9 H5
Lydwell Cl DT4 54 B2
Lym Cl DT7 35 E3
Lyme Rd DT7 35 A1
Lyme Regis 12 B3
Lyme Regis
 Golf Club DT7 35 F1
Lyme Regis Ind Est DT7 35 C2
Lyme Regis
 Leisure Centre DT7 35 D3
Lyme Regis
 Marine Aquarium DT7 35 D4
Lymes Cl DT4 54 B4
Lynch La DT4 54 A2
Lynch Rd DT4 54 B2
Lyndhurst Rd,
 Christchurch BH23 29 G2
Lyndhurst Rd,
 Weymouth DT4 52 D5
Lynmoor Rd DT4 53 E4
Lyon's Gate 9 G6
Lyons Walk SP7 40 C3
Lysander Cl DT3 29 H3
Lytchett Matravers 14 C2
Lytchett Minster 14 C2
Lytchett Minster
 By-Pass BH16 37 B3
Lytchett Rd BH16 46 C3
Lyte's Cary Manor(NT) 9 E3
Lytton Rd BH1 21 E3

M

Mabel Gale Homes DT6 22 C5
Macaulay Rd BH18 27 F4
Macville Av BH20 58 D3
Madeira Rd BH1 20 C4
Madison Av BH1 21 F2
Maen Gdns DT1 31 F4
Magdalen Ct DT6 22 B3
Magdalen La,
 Bridport DT6 22 B4
Magdalen La,
 Christchurch BH23 28 A4
Magdalene La SP7 40 B3
Magnolia Cl,
 Bournemouth BH6 28 A6
Magnolia Cl,
 Verwood BH31 49 F4
Magnolia Cl,
 Weymouth DT3 48 D6
Maiden Castle 13 G3
Maiden Castle Cotts DT2 30 C6
Maiden Castle Rd DT2 30 B6
Maiden Newton 13 F2
Maiden St DT4 55 F2
Main Rd, Portland DT5 32 C1
Main Rd,
 West Lulworth BH20 51 B2
Main St,
 Bothenhampton DT6 23 D5
Main St, Dorchester DT2 17 B5
Mallams DT5 32 B3
Mallard Cl BH23 29 G4
Mallory Cl BH23 29 F2
Mallow Cl BH23 29 H2
Malmesbury Cl BH23 28 E2
Malmesbury Ct BH8 21 E2
Malmesbury House 11 G3
Malmesbury Park Pl BH8 21 E2
Malmesbury Park Rd
 BH8 22 D2
Maloren Way BH22 56 C5
Malta Cl DT1 30 C2
Malthouse BH15 38 B5
Malvern Cl*,
 Dorset Rd BH23 29 E2
Malvern Ter DT4 54 C2
Mampitts La SP7 40 E3
Mampitts Rd SP7 40 D3
Mandalay Cl BH23 49 B4
Mandeville Cl DT4 54 B4
Mandeville Rd DT4 54 A4
Manningford Rd DT11 19 B2
Mannington 10 D6
Mannington Pl*,
 West Hill Rd BH2 20 A5
Manor Av DT7 35 D2
Manor Barn DT6 24 C3
Manor Ct DT9 41 D2
Manor Farm Cl,
 Blandford Forum DT11 18 A1
Manor Farm Cl,
 Dorchester DT2 37 C5
Manor Farm Rd BH20 17 B2
Manor Flds DT6 22 E4
Manor Gdns,
 Beaminster DT8 16 C5
Manor Gdns,
 Swanage BH19 45 E4
Manor Gdns,
 Verwood BH31 49 B2
Manor La BH31 49 B3
Manor Pk BH15 38 A2
Manor Rd,
 Bournemouth BH1 21 E5
Manor Rd,
 Christchurch BH23 28 A4
Manor Rd,
 Dorchester DT1 31 E5
Manor Rd,
 Swanage BH19 45 G5
Manor Rd,
 Verwood BH31 49 B2
Manor Way DT3 52 B2
Manor Way BH31 49 C2
Manston 10 A5
Manston Rd DT10 43 C5
Manswood 10 C6
Mantle Cl DT5 32 C2
Manton Cl BH15 47 D2
Manton Rd BH15 47 D2
Manwell Dr BH19 45 F5
Manwell Rd BH19 45 F5

Manwells La BH21 45 F4
Maple Cl SP7 40 D1
Maple Gdns DT6 23 C5
Maple Rd BH15 38 C4
Maple Row DT10 43 C2
Maple Way SP8 34 B4
Mapperton 13 E1
Mapperton House
 Gardens 13 E1
Mappowder 9 H6
Marabout Cl BH23 28 D3
Marabout Ind Est DT1 30 D2
Margards La BH31 49 A3
Margaret Pl DT1 30 C4
Marian Cl BH21 27 A4
Marian Rd BH21 27 A4
Marie Rd DT1 30 C4
Marina Cl BH5 21 G5
Marina Ct BH5 21 G5
Marina Gdns DT4 54 D3
Marina Towers BH5 21 G5
Marina Vw BH23 28 A5
Marine Par DT7 35 D4
Marine Theatre DT7 35 E3
Mariners Cl BH23 29 F5
Mariners Dr BH19 45 F5
Mariners Way DT3 26 C1
Market Cl, Poole BH15 38 B5
Market Cl,
 Wareham BH20 50 C6
Market Cross DT10 43 B6
Market Cross Mews
 DT10 43 B6
Market Pl,
 Blandford Forum DT11 19 B5
Market Pl,
 Sherborne DT9 41 D3
Market Pl,
 Sturminster Newton
 DT10 43 B6
Market St, Poole BH15 38 A6
Market St,
 Weymouth DT4 55 F4
Market Way BH21 57 C4
Markham Av DT4 54 C3
Marlborough Av DT4 54 C6
Marlborough Cl BH21 57 B2
Marlborough Pl BH21 57 C2
Marlborough Rd BH4 20 A5
Marley Cl DT3 39 C2
Marlott Rd,
 Gillingham SP8 34 B1
Marlott Rd, Poole BH15 38 B2
Marlow Rd DT4 55 F3
Marmion Grn BH23 29 E3
Marnhull 10 A4
Marnhull Rd BH15 38 C3
Marquis Cl DT4 54 A2
Marrowbone La DT6 23 E6
Marsh Barn Rd DT6 23 C8
Marsh Ditch BH23 28 A5
Marsh Gate DT6 23 C6
Marsh La,
 Christchurch BH23 28 D4
Marsh La, Poole BH16 46 B2
Marsh Rd DT4 55 E2
Marsh Way,
 Blandford Forum DT11 18 A1
Marsh Way,
 Swanage BH19 45 E4
Marshall Row BH19 45 G4
Marshallsay Ct DT3 26 B1
Marshallsay Rd DT3 26 B1
Marshlands Cl BH23 28 D4
Marsh's Ct DT11 19 B4
Marshwood 12 C1
Marshwood Rd DT1 31 F4
Marston Cl DT11 19 B3
Marston Rd, Poole BH15 38 A5
Marston Rd,
 Sherborne DT9 41 A1
Martel Cl DT2 17 A6
Martin Cl DT1 19 D3
Martingale Cl BH16 46 E2
Martins Hill Cl BH21 28 C1
Martins Hill La BH23 28 C1
Martinscroft Rd DT5 33 A7
Martinstown 13 F3
Martleaves Cl DT4 54 B2
Martyr Cl DT1 30 C6
Mary Cossins Cl DT11 19 B2
Mary La BH22 56 A4
Maryland Rd BH16 47 B1
Maskew Cl DT3 26 B2

Masterson Cl BH23 28 D3
Matchams Karting 15 E1
Matthews Pl SP8 34 C2
Maud Rd DT1 30 D4
Maumbury Rd DT1 31 E4
Maumbury Rings DT1 31 E4
Maunsel Av DT3 39 B2
Mawdwalls DT3 39 C2
Max Gate (N.T) DT1 31 H4
May Terrace Gdns DT3 26 B1
Maycroft Rd DT4 55 E3
Mayfield Cl DT4 52 A5
McCreery Rd DT9 41 D1
McKay Cl DT4 54 A2
McKay Way DT4 54 A2
Mdws Cl BH16 46 D2
Mead Flds DT6 22 A2
Mead La DT6 22 A2
Mead Rd,
 Wareham BH20 26 C6
Mead Rd,
 Weymouth DT4 52 A4
Meaders Yd DT10 43 B1
Meadow Bank BH16 46 D2
Meadow Cl,
 Shaftesbury SP7 40 D2
Meadow Cl,
 Sturminster Newton
 DT10 43 C2
Meadow Cl,
 Weymouth DT3 26 B2
Meadow Ct,
 Bridport DT6 22 D4
Meadow Ct,
 Verwood BH31 49 D4
Meadow Ct,
 Wimborne BH21 57 C4
Meadow Gro BH31 49 D3
Meadow La BH20 58 C2
Meadow Rd DT11 19 C5
Meadow Rise BH18 27 D3
Meadow View Cl BH20 50 C6
Meadow View Rd BH23 48 B4
Meadow Vw,
 Blandford Forum DT11 19 C5
Meadow Vw,
 Charminster DT2 25 B3
Meadow Vw,
 Dorchester DT1 31 E2
Meadow Way,
 Bridport DT6 25 C5
Meadow Way,
 Verwood BH31 49 D3
Meadowcroft SP8 34 D4
Meadowland BH23 29 E4
Meadowlands DT6 23 C7
Meadows Dr BH16 46 D2
Meadowsweet Rd BH17 46 F1
Meadway DT6 23 A8
Meare Fish House 8 D1
Medbourne Cl DT11 19 B3
Medlar Cl BH23 28 D1
Medway Dr DT3 39 B3
Meech Cl DT6 23 C6
Melbourne Rd BH8 21 F2
Melbourne St DT4 54 C1
Melbury Abbas 10 B4
Melbury Bubb 9 F6
Melbury Ct*,
 Cranborne Rd BH19 45 G4
Melbury Osmond 9 E6
Melbury Rd BH19 55 E1
Melbury Sampford 9 E6
Melbury Way SP7 40 E3
Melchester Cl SP8 34 C1
Melcombe Av DT4 53 E5
Melcombe Bingham 13 H1
Melcombe Pl DT4 53 E6
Melcombe Regis 13 G5
Mellstock Av DT3 31 E6
Mellstock Cres BH20 50 A4
Mellstock Rd BH15 38 B2
Melplash 12 D2
Melstock Av DT3 53 G1
Melstock Cl DT11 19 D2
Melstock Rd SP8 34 B1
Melverley Gdns BH21 57 C2
Melville Sq DT6 22 D4
Melway Gdns DT11 42 C3
Melway La DT11 42 C3
Mendip Cl BH31 49 C3
Mendip Ct*,
 Dorset Rd BH23 29 E2
Mendip Rd BH31 49 C2
Menin Rd BH20 24 A5

Mercery Rd DT3 52 C3
Mere Museum 10 A2
Meredith Cl BH23 28 D3
Mereside DT5 32 A1
Merino Way BH22 56 B5
Merlewood Cl BH2 20 B3
Merley **14 D2**
Merley House La BH21 57 C6
Merley Rd DT4 54 C6
Merley Ways BH21 57 C5
Merlin Av North DT3 48 A5
Merlin Av South DT3 48 A5
Merlin Way BH23 29 G5
Mermaid Ct BH5 21 G5
Mermond Pl BH19 45 G4
Merredin Cl DT3 48 C5
Merrivale DT1 30 B3
Merryfield Cl BH31 49 C2
Merton Ter .DT5 32 C3
Methuen Cl BH8 21 E3
Methuen Cl BH8 20 D2
Methuen Rd BH8 20 D2
Meyrick Park Cres BH3 20 B2
Meyrick Pk BH4 20 A3
Meyrick Rd BH1 20 D5
Michelgrove Rd BH5 21 G5
Middle Bere Dr BH20 50 A3
Middle Farm Way DT1 30 B4
Middle Grn DT8 16 C5
Middle Rd,
  Lytchett Matravers
  BH16 36 B4
Middle Rd, Poole BH15 38 D1
Middle St,
  Burton Bradstock DT6 24 B2
Middle St,
  St Andrews Well DT6 22 F1
Middlebere Cres BH16 47 B2
Middlemarsh **9 G6**
Middlemarsh St DT1 30 C3
Midelney Manor 8 C3
Midleaze DT9 41 A4
Milborne St Andrew **14 A2**
Miles Av BH20 50 C1
Miles Gdns DT3 48 A3
Milestone Rd BH16 38 C1
Milestone Way SP8 34 B3
Milford Cl BH22 56 C4
Milford Court Mews SP8 34 A3
Milford Ct SP8 34 A3
Milford Rd DT1 30 D4
Mill Grn DT7 35 E3
Mill House
  Cider Museum 14 A3
Mill La, Dorchester DT2 25 C3
Mill La, Lyme Regis DT7 35 E3
Mill La, Uplyme DT7 35 B1
Mill La, Wareham BH20 50 B5
Mill La, Weymouth DT3 39 C2
Mill La, Wimborne BH21 57 B3
Mill Pl SP7 40 C3
Mill Race SP8 34 D2
Mill Rd BH23 28 A2
Mill St, Bridport DT6 24 B2
Mill St, Dorchester DT1 31 G3
Mill St, Puddletown DT2 39 B5
Mill St, Weymouth DT3 48 A5
Mill Ter DT6 24 B2
Millbrook Cl DT11 42 C1
Millbrook Ct DT11 42 C1
Milldown Rd DT11 19 A1
Miller Rd BH23 28 D3
Miller Way*,
  Dunston St DT9 41 E2
Millers Cl,
  Dorchester DT1 31 E2
Millers Cl,
  Weymouth DT3 39 C2
Millfield DT8 16 B4
Millhams St BH23 28 B4
Millhams St North BH23 28 B4
Millom La DT2 39 B6
Millstream Cl BH21 57 B3
Millstream Mews BH23 28 B3
Milton Abbas **14 A1**
Milton Abbey 14 A1
Milton Cl DT4 52 D4
Milton Cres DT4 52 D4
Milton Manor House 14 A1
Milton on Stour **10 A3**
Milton Rd,
  Bournemouth BH1 20 C3
Milton Rd,
  Weymouth DT4 54 D1

Milton Rd,
  Wimborne BH21 57 B1
Milton Ter DT4 52 D4
Minerva Cl DT1 30 D5
Miniature
  Golf Course DT4 53 E4
Minster Vw BH21 57 C2
Minster Way BH16 46 C2
Minterne Gardens 13 G1
Minterne Magna **13 G1**
Minterne Rd BH23 29 E5
Minton Pl DT4 52 C6
Mission Hall La DT3 39 D1
Mistover Cl DT1 31 E6
Mistover Rd BH20 50 A4
Mitchell St*, East St DT4 55 F2
Mithras Cl DT1 30 C5
Mixen La DT1 31 G5
Miz-Maze 11 F4
Model Town & Gdns
  BH21 57 A3
Model Village BH20 26 B4
Moffat Rd BH23 28 D4
Mohune Way DT3 26 C2
Mompesson House (NT) 11 G3
Moneyfly Rd BH31 49 E3
Monkey World Ape
  Rescue Centre 14 B3
Monks Cl BH22 56 B6
Monkshood Cl BH23 29 H1
Monkswell Grn BH23 28 C4
Monkton Down Rd DT11 18 C6
Monkton Hill DT2 30 D6
Monkton Up
Wimborne **10 D5**
Monmouth Av DT3 52 D3
Monmouth Cl BH31 49 E4
Monmouth Dr BH31 49 E4
Monmouth Gdns DT8 16 B4
Monmouth Rd,
  Dorchester DT1 31 E5
Monmouth Rd,
  Wareham BH20 50 B6
Monmouth St DT7 35 E3
Monnington La DT1 30 B3
Montacute House (NT) 9 E4
Montrose Cl,
  Portland DT5 33 C6
Montrose Cl,
  Verwood BH31 49 C2
Moor Rd,
  Broadstone BH18 27 F3
Moor Rd, Swanage BH19 45 F1
Moor View Rd BH15 38 D1
Moorcombe Dr DT3 39 B2
Moordown **15 E2**
Moordown Av DT3 53 F2
Moorfield Rd DT5 33 D6
Moorings Cl BH15 47 F4
Moorland Cres BH16 46 C3
Moorland Par BH16 46 C2
Moorland Rd BH1 21 F4
Moorland Way BH16 46 C3
Moorlands Rd,
  Ferndown BH22 56 A4
Moorlands Rd,
  Verwood BH31 49 C1
Moorlands Rise BH22 56 B3
Moors Valley
  Country Park 11 E6
Moorside Av DT4 53 E3
Moorside Cl DT4 53 E3
Moorside Rd,
  Ferndown BH22 56 A5
Moorside Rd,
  Wimborne BH21 27 B3
Moraston St DT1 30 B3
Moray Ct BH21 57 B3
Morcombelake **12 C2**
Morden Bog NNR 14 B3
Morden Rd BH20 50 C1
More Crichel **10 D6**
Moreton **14 A3**
Moreton Rd,
  Dorchester DT2 51 C5
Moreton Rd,
  Wareham BH20 58 A2
Moretons La BH20 50 C5
Moreys Cl BH20 51 C1
Moriconium Quay BH15 47 C4
Morris Rd BH20 24 D5
Morrison Rd BH19 45 E4
Mortain Cl DT11 19 B2
Mortimer Cl BH23 29 G4

Mosterton **12 D1**
Motcombe **10 A3**
Motcombe Rd SP7 40 C1
Mount Batten Cl BH23 29 F5
Mount Pleasant
  Av North DT3 52 B2
Mount Pleasant
  Av South DT3 52 C3
Mount Pleasant Bsns Pk
  DT3 52 C2
Mount Pleasant La BH19 45 G4
Mount Pleasant Rd
  BH15 38 C5
Mount Pleasant,
  Bridport DT6 22 B3
Mount Pleasant,
  Swanage BH19 44 A4
Mount Pleasant,
  Wareham BH20 50 B5
Mount Scars BH19 45 G4
Mount Skippet Way DT2 51 B6
Mount St DT4 55 F3
Mount Stuart Rd BH5 21 G5
Mountain Ash Rd DT1 30 D3
Mountbatten Cl DT4 54 B4
Mountjoy DT6 23 C6
Mowlem Ct*,
  Rempstone Rd BH19 45 G4
Moynton Cl DT2 51 B5
Moynton Rd DT1 31 F5
Muchelney Abbey (EH) 8 C3
Mude Gdns BH23 29 F5
Mudeford Grn Cl BH23 29 F5
Mudeford La BH23 29 E4
Mudeford, **15 F3**
Mudeford,
  Christchurch BH23 29 E5
Mudros Rd BH11 18 C4
Mulberry Av DT5 32 B2
Mulberry Cl SP8 34 D2
Mulberry Gdns DT9 41 C2
Mulberry Ter*,
  School St DT4 55 F1
Museum of Electricity
  BH23 28 B3
Museum of
  South Somerset 9 E5
Mustons La SP7 40 C3
Myrtle Cl DT8 16 B5
Myrtle Rd BH8 21 F2

N

Nairn Rd BH3 20 B2
Nansen Av BH15 38 C2
Nantillo St DT1 30 B3
Napier Rd BH15 47 A3
Nathan Gdns BH15 47 D3
Neacroft **15 F2**
Nelson Dr BH23 29 F5
Nelson Rd BH11 18 C5
Nether Cerne **13 G2**
Nether Compton **9 F4**
Netherbury **12 D1**
Nethercoombe La DT9 41 B2
Netherton Rd DT4 55 E4
Netherton St DT1 30 B4
Netherwood Pl BH21 57 A2
Netmead La DT11 42 A1
Nettlebed Nursery SP7 40 B2
Nettlecombe **13 E2**
Nettlecombe,
  Shaftesbury SP7 40 D2
New Bond St DT4 55 F2
New Borough Rd BH21 57 C4
New Buildings Rd BH20 58 A3
New Church Cl DT5 33 D6
New Cl DT4 54 B5
New Close Gdns DT4 55 E4
New Forest Museum 11 H6
New Forest
  Owl Sanctuary 15 F1
New Forest Reptiliary 11 H6
New Forest Water Park 11 F6
New Ground DT5 32 C4
New Harbour Rd BH15 38 A6
New Harbour Rd South
  BH15 38 A6
New Harbour Rd West
  BH15 38 A6
New La SP7 40 F4
New Orch BH15 38 A5
New Quay Rd BH15 38 A6

New Rd,
  Blandford Forum DT11 19 A5
New Rd,
  Bovington Camp BH20 24 B4
New Rd, Dorchester DT2 30 C1
New Rd, Gillingham SP8 34 D4
New Rd, Poole BH16 37 C1
New Rd, Portland DT5 32 B4
New Rd,
  Shaftesbury SP7 40 A2
New Rd,
  Sherbourne DT9 41 D4
New Rd,
  Sturminster Newton
  DT10 43 C1
New Rd, Weymouth DT4 55 E2
New Rd, Wool BH20 58 B3
New Sherborne Castle
  DT9 41 F3
New St, Dorchester DT1 31 E3
New St, Poole BH15 38 B6
New St, Portland DT5 32 B4
New St, Puddletown DT2 39 B6
New St, Wareham BH20 50 B6
New St, Weymouth DT4 55 F2
New Zealand Ter DT6 22 C4
Newberry Gdns DT4 55 F3
Newberry Rd DT4 55 F3
Newbury Gdns SP8 34 D3
Newbury SP8 34 E3
Newcombe Rd BH22 56 A4
Newcroft Gdns BH23 28 A2
Newell DT9 41 C3
Newfield Rd DT11 18 A1
Newfoundland Dr BH15 38 B5
Newfoundland DT6 22 F1
Newland DT9 41 D3
Newland Gdn DT9 41 E3
Newlands Rd BH23 29 F3
Newman Cl DT11 19 C3
Newmans Cl,
  Ferndown BH22 56 A1
Newmans Cl,
  Wimborne BH21 57 C5
Newmans La BH22 56 A1
Newstead Rd DT4 52 C6
Newton Cl SP8 34 B3
Newton Ct BH19 45 E4
Newton Manor Cl BH19 45 E4
Newton Rd,
  Dorchester DT2 37 C6
Newton Rd,
  Swanage BH19 45 G5
Newton Rise BH19 45 E4
Newtons Rd DT4 55 F3
Newtown La BH31 49 C3
Newtown Rd BH31 49 D2
Newtown, **14 D2**
Newtown,
  Beaminster DT8 16 B4
Nicodemus Knob DT5 32 E3
Nightingale Cl BH31 49 D3
Nightingale Ct DT11 19 B4
Nightingale Dr DT3 48 B4
Nightjar Cl BH17 46 F2
Nine Stones 13 F3
Noake Rd DT9 41 B4
Nonesuch Cl DT1 31 G5
Noon Gdns BH31 49 E2
Noon Hill Dr BH31 49 E2
Noon Hill Rd BH31 49 E2
Norburton DT6 24 C2
Norden **14 C4**
Norden Dr BH20 50 C4
Norden La DT2 37 C5
Nordon Rd DT11 19 C3
Nordons DT6 23 D5
Norfolk Cl DT6 22 D4
Norfolk Rd DT4 54 C1
Norman Cl DT6 22 E3
Normandy Dr BH23 28 D3
Normandy Way,
  Bridport DT6 22 C4
Normandy Way,
  Dorchester DT1 30 C3
Normandy Way,
  Poole BH15 47 C3
Normanton Down 11 E1
North Allington DT6 22 B2
North Av DT7 35 D2
North Bestwall Rd BH20 50 D5
North Causeway BH20 50 B5
North Hill Cl DT6 24 B2

North Hill Way DT6 23 C6
North Mills Rd DT6 22 C2
North Mills Trading Est
  DT6 22 C2
North Pl DT11 19 B4
North Quay DT4 55 E2
North Rd,
  Bournemouth BH1 21 H3
North Rd,
  Dorchester DT2 37 C5
North Rd,
  Sherbourne DT9 41 D2
North Rd,
  Weymouth DT4 54 B4
North Sq,
  Dorchester DT1 31 E3
North Sq,
  Weymouth DT3 26 B1
North St,
  Beaminster DT8 16 C5
North St,
  Bere Regis BH20 17 C2
North St, Bridport DT6 22 C3
North St, Dorchester DT2 22 C3
North St, Poole BH15 38 B5
North St, Wareham BH20 50 B5
North Walls BH20 50 B5
North Wootton **9 G5**
Northbrook Rd BH19 45 F1
Northcote Rd BH1 21 E4
Northernhay DT1 31 E2
Northfields DT10 43 C4
Northmoor Way BH20 50 A3
Northover Cl DT6 24 C1
Northport Dr BH20 50 B3
Nortoft Rd BH8 20 D2
Norton Cl BH23 28 D3
Norton Way BH15 47 F4
Norwich Av BH2 20 A5
Norwich Av West BH2 20 A5
Norwich Rd,
  Bournemouth BH2 20 A5
Norwich Rd,
  Weymouth DT4 55 E3
Nothe Fort DT4 55 G2
Nothe Gdns DT4 55 G2
Nothe Par DT4 55 G2
Nothe Walk DT4 55 G2
Nottington **13 G4**
Nottington La DT3 48 A6
Nugent Rd BH23 28 A6
Nundico BH20 50 C5
Nursery Gdns DT6 22 C4
Nursery Rd DT11 19 B4
Nutcombe Cl DT6 25 B4
Nutcombe Ter DT6 25 B4
Nutgrove Av DT4 54 B3
Nuthatch Cl DT3 48 C5
Nuthatch Cl BH1 21 G3
Nutmead Cl DT11 42 C1

O

Oak Cl BH21 27 B3
Oak Dr BH15 38 C5
Oak Rd,
  Bournemouth BH8 21 F2
Oak Rd,
  Fordingbridge SP6 16 B3
Oak Rd, Poole BH16 46 D3
Oak Vw DT11 19 C4
Oak Way DT3 53 G2
Oakbury Dr DT3 53 G2
Oakdale Rd BH15 38 D1
Oakdene Cl BH21 57 D3
Oakdene Rd BH20 58 B3
Oake Woods SP8 34 D4
Oakfield Ct*,
  Oakfield St DT11 19 B4
Oakfield Rd BH15 38 B1
Oakfield St DT11 19 B4
Oakhurst Cl BH22 56 B4
Oakhurst La BH22 56 B4
Oakhurst Rd BH22 56 B4
Oaklands Cl BH31 49 B2
Oakley Gdns BH16 46 B2
Oakley Hill BH21 57 C5
Oakley La BH21 57 D6
Oakley Pl DT4 55 F3
Oakley Rd BH21 57 D6
Oakley Straight BH21 57 D6
Oaks Mead BH31 49 C2
Oakwood DT2 17 C4
Oasis Mews BH16 46 B2

Oban Rd BH3 20 B1
Oborne 9 G4
Oborne Rd DT9 41 E3
Ocean Heights BH5 21 H5
Oceanarium BH2 20 C6
Octagon Theatre 9 E5
October Pl BH8 21 E1
Odeon Cinema BH1 20 C5
Okeford Fitzpaine 10 A6
Okeford Row DT11 42 B6
Old Bakery Cl DT11 18 A3
Old Barn Farm Rd BH21 56 D1
Old Barn Rd BH20 17 B2
Old Bincombe La DT3 39 C1
Old Bound Rd BH16 46 D4
Old Boundary Rd SP7 40 D3
Old Bri Ct*, Newstead Rd DT4 54 E1
Old Brickfields DT2 17 C5
Old Castle Rd DT4 55 E5
Old Chalk Pit BH20 17 B3
Old Chapel Dr BH16 36 C2
Old Christchurch La*, Old Christchurch Rd BH1 20 C5
Old Christchurch Rd BH1 20 B5
Old Church Rd DT6 23 D6
Old Crown Court & Cells DT1 31 E3
Old Depot Rd DT5 32 D1
Old Farm Ct DT11 19 C2
Old Farm East & West DT9 41 C3
Old Farm Gdns DT11 19 C2
Old Farm Rd BH15 38 D1
Old Farm Way DT2 51 B5
Old Forge Cl, Fordingbridge SP6 16 B2
Old Forge Cl, Poole BH16 37 C2
Old Granary Cl DT3 39 C2
Old Highway Mews BH21 57 D3
Old Hill DT5 32 C3
Old Kiln Rd BH16 46 E3
Old Laundry Trading Est DT6 22 D3
Old Lyme Hill DT6 25 A5
Old Lyme Rd DT6 25 A5
Old Manor Cl BH21 57 D3
Old Market Hill DT10 43 B5
Old Market Mews DT10 43 B2
Old Mkt Centre Ind Est SP8 34 D3
Old Orch BH15 38 B6
Old Parish La DT4 54 D1
Old Pound Cl BH16 36 B2
Old Rd BH21 57 A3
Old Rectory Cl DT6 25 C5
Old Rectory Mews BH15 47 E4
Old Roman Rd DT3 48 A1
Old Rope Walks DT6 22 C2
Old Sarum (EH) 11 F2
Old Sawmill Cl BH31 49 A2
Old School Pl DT9 41 C4
Old Sherborne Castle DT9 41 F3
Old Station Rd DT3 48 A4
Old Town Mews*, Market Cl BH15 38 B5
Old Vicarage Cl DT2 25 C2
Old Vicarage Gdn DT7 35 D3
Old Wardour Castle (EH) 10 C3
Old Watery La BH16 37 C2
Olga Rd DT1 30 D4
Olivers Mead DT11 42 B1
Onslow Gdns BH21 57 C2
Onslow Ho BH21 57 C2
Ophir Gdns BH8 21 E3
Ophir Rd BH8 20 D3
Orch St BH2 20 B5
Orchard Av DT6 22 B2
Orchard Cl, Bridport DT6 25 C5
Orchard Cl, Christchurch BH23 28 A4
Orchard Cl, Poole BH16 37 B2
Orchard Cl, Wimborne BH21 27 B1
Orchard Cres DT6 22 B2
Orchard Ct, Bournemouth BH1 21 F4
Orchard Ct, Verwood BH31 49 D3
Orchard Dr DT3 53 G1
Orchard La BH21 27 B1
Orchard Mews, Christchurch BH23 28 A4
Orchard Mews, Gillingham SP8 34 B3
Orchard Rd SP8 34 C2
Orchard St, Blandford Forum DT11 19 B4
Orchard St, Dorchester DT1 31 F2
Orcheston Rd BH8 21 E2
Orchid Way BH23 28 C3
Orford St DT2 39 B5
Orion Rd DT4 55 E3
Osborne Cl DT1 31 G4
Osborne Rd, Portland DT5 32 B2
Osborne Rd, Swanage BH19 45 F5
Osborne Rd, Wimborne BH21 57 C4
Osborne Ter*, Osborne Rd DT5 32 B2
Osbourne Rd DT6 22 C3
Osmay Rd BH19 45 G6
Osmington 13 H4
Osmington Dro DT2 17 B6
Osmington Hill DT3 39 D2
Osmington Mills 13 H4
Osprey Cl BH23 29 F5
Osprey Quay Bsns Pk DT5 32 A1
Otter Cl, Poole BH16 46 C3
Otter Cl, Verwood BH31 49 D3
Ottery La DT9 41 C4
Overbury Cl DT4 54 B2
Overcombe Cotts DT3 53 H2
Overcombe Dr DT3 53 H1
Overlands Rd DT4 54 B4
Overton Cl DT7 35 E1
Overton Walk DT11 19 B3
Owermoigne 13 H4
Owl Ct BH20 17 B2
Owls Rd, Bournemouth BH5 21 G4
Owls Rd, Verwood BH31 49 D3
Oxencroft SP7 40 D2
Oxford Pl DT6 22 C3
Oxford Rd BH8 20 D4
Oxford Ter*, Richmond Rd BH19 45 F4
Ozone Ter DT7 35 D4

P

Paceycombe Way DT1 30 B3
Paddock Cl, Poole BH16 36 D2
Paddock Cl, Shaftesbury SP7 40 E4
Paddock Gro BH31 49 D3
Pageant Cl*, Pageant Dr DT9 41 D4
Pageant Dr DT9 41 D4
Pageant Gardens DT9 41 D4
Pageants Cl DT6 22 E1
Palace Rd SP8 34 E3
Palm Ct DT3 52 C3
Palmer Rd BH15 38 B2
Palmers Orch BH16 36 C3
Palmerston Av BH23 28 D4
Palmerston Cl BH16 46 E2
Palmerston Mews BH1 21 G3
Palmerston Rd, Bournemouth BH1 21 G3
Palmerston Rd, Poole BH16 46 D2
Panorama Rd BH19 45 E4
Paradise St BH15 38 A6
Paris Ct SP8 34 D3
Parish Rd BH15 38 D4
Park Ct DT3 48 D6
Park Dr, Dorchester DT2 51 B4
Park Dr, Verwood BH31 49 B1
Park Estate Rd DT5 33 C6
Park Gdns BH23 29 E4
Park Gro DT10 43 B2
Park La, Fordingbridge SP6 16 B2
Park La, Shaftesbury SP7 40 C3
Park La, Weymouth DT4 52 D5
Park La, Wimborne BH21 57 B3
Park Lake Rd BH15 38 D5
Park Lands DT11 19 A4
Park Mead Rd DT4 54 C6
Park Pl, Blandford Forum DT11 19 B4
Park Pl, Bournemouth BH8 21 E1
Park Rd, Blandford Forum DT11 19 B3
Park Rd, Bournemouth BH8 20 D3
Park Rd, Bridport DT6 22 B3
Park Rd, Portland DT5 33 D6
Park Rd, Sturminster Newton DT10 43 B2
Park Rd, Swanage BH19 45 G5
Park St DT4 55 F1
Park View Ct BH15 38 C4
Park Walk SP7 40 B3
Park Way BH22 56 A4
Parkside Ct DT3 48 D6
Parkstone 14 D3
Parkstone Rd BH15 38 C4
Parkway DT6 25 C5
Parkwood Rd BH21 57 C3
Parley Cross 15 E2
Parr Gro DT11 18 A2
Parr Way DT4 55 E5
Parsonage Down NNR 10 D1
Parsonage Rd, Bournemouth BH1 20 C5
Parsonage Rd, Bridport DT6 22 B2
Parsons Cl BH19 45 G1
Parsons Pool SP7 40 C2
Partridge Cl BH23 29 F5
Pasture Way DT6 23 D5
Patchins Rd BH16 47 A2
Paul Baker's La DT11 18 A2
Pauls Mead DT5 32 C3
Pauls Way DT2 51 B5
Paultons Park 11 H5
Pauntley Rd BH23 29 E4
Pavilion Complex DT4 55 F2
Pavilion Theatre 13 G5
Payne Cl BH22 56 B1
Peacemarsh Farm Cl SP8 34 C1
Peacemarsh SP8 34 C1
Peacemarsh Ter SP8 34 C1
Pear Tree Cl SP6 16 B2
Pearce Rd BH16 46 C3
Peatons La BH16 36 A1
Pebble La DT5 32 B2
Peel Cl, Blandford Forum DT11 19 C3
Peel Cl, Verwood BH31 49 B1
Peelers Ct DT6 22 D3
Pegasus Ct BH1 20 C3
Pelham Cl BH23 28 D4
Pemberton Cl DT3 48 C5
Penbugle Yd DT1 30 B3
Pendruffle La DT1 30 B4
Penhale Walk*, Briston Cl DT1 30 B4
Penn Ct BH22 56 A4
Pennant Way BH23 29 F3
Pennine Ct BH23 29 F2
Pennine Way BH31 49 C3
Pennington Cl BH22 56 A5
Pennington Cres BH22 56 A5
Pennington Rd BH22 56 A5
Pennsylvania Rd DT5 33 D7
Penny Plot DT7 35 C3
Penny St DT10 43 B6
Penny St*, Hardwick St DT4 52 D6
Penrith Cl BH31 49 B3
Penrose Cl BH16 36 C4
Pentridge 10 D4
Pepper Hill DT11 42 B6
Peppercorn Cl BH23 28 D2
Perbeck Terrace Rd BH19 45 G5
Percy Gdns DT11 19 C4
Percy Rd BH5 21 G4
Peregrine Rd BH23 29 F5
Perry Gdns BH15 38 B6
Perryfields Quarry Butterfly Reserve DT5 33 D7
Perry's Cider Mill 8 B5
Perth St DT4 54 C1
Peters Cl BH16 46 D3
Peverell Av East DT1 30 B3
Peverell Av West DT1 30 A3
Peverell Rd BH16 47 A2
Peveril Hghts BH19 45 H5
Peveril Point Rd BH19 45 H5
Peveril Rd BH19 45 H5
Pheasant Way SP8 34 E4
Phelips Rd BH21 27 C1
Philip Rd DT11 19 D3
Philipp's House & Dinton Park (NT) 10 D2
Phippard Way BH15 38 C5
Piddlehinton 13 H2
Piddlehinton Rd DT2 31 G2
Piddletrenthide 13 H1
Pier App BH2 20 C6
Pier Ter DT6 23 B8
Pier Theatre BH2 20 C6
Pigeon Cl DT11 19 B6
Pilgrims Way DT4 55 F2
Pilsdon 12 C2
Pilsdon Cl DT8 16 A5
Pilsdon Pen 12 C1
Pimperne 10 C6
Pimpernel Ct SP8 34 B3
Pine Mansions BH1 21 F4
Pine Rd SP6 16 B2
Pine Ridge DT7 35 E2
Pine Tree Cl BH21 57 D3
Pine View Cl BH31 49 A2
Pine View Rd BH31 49 A2
Pine Vw Cl BH16 46 D3
Pine Vw DT6 22 A4
Pine Walk, Ferndown BH22 56 B3
Pine Walk, Lyme Regis DT7 35 D4
Pine Walk, Shaftesbury SP7 40 B3
Pine Walk, Verwood BH31 49 E3
Pinehurst Av BH23 29 F5
Pinehurst Rd BH22 56 A5
Pinemoor Cl DT3 53 F2
Pines Ct DT11 19 C4
Pines Mews DT8 16 B5
Pinewood Cl BH16 46 B2
Pinewood Ct BH22 56 A4
Pinewood Rd BH16 46 B2
Pinford La DT9 41 F3
Pipers Dr BH23 29 G3
Pipit Cl DT3 48 C4
Pipit Ct BH15 38 B5
Pirate Adventure Golf DT4 53 F4
Pirates La DT4 54 B6
Pitcote La DT1 30 B3
Pitt Cl DT11 19 B6
Pitts Orch DT10 43 B5
Pitwines Cl BH15 38 B5
Pix Mead Gdns SP7 40 E4
Plaisters La DT3 39 C1
Plantagenet Way SP8 34 A3
Plantation Cl BH19 45 E5
Plassey Cl DT1 30 C2
Plaza Cinema DT1 31 E3
Plough Est DT11 19 C2
Plover Dr DT3 26 B2
Plumtree Gdns DT6 22 D4
Plush 13 H1
Podington Mdws DT3 26 C1
Polden Hills 8 D2
Policemans La BH16 46 A2
Pond Walk DT10 43 B2
Pony Dr BH16 46 E2
Poole 14 D3
Poole Arts Centre 14 D3
Poole Harbour BH15 47 A4
Poole Hill BH2 20 A5
Poole Hospital BH15 38 C4
Poole Pottery BH15 38 B6
Poole Rd, Bournemouth BH4 20 A5
Poole Rd, Lytchett Matravers BH16 36 F1
Poole Rd, Upton BH16 46 D2
Poole Rd, Wimborne BH21 57 C3
Poole Stadium BH15 38 B3
Pooles Ct DT7 35 E3
Poorton 13 E2
Popes Rd BH15 38 C1
Poplar Cl*, West St BH15 38 A6
Poplar Cl, Weymouth DT4 52 A4
Poplar Cl, Wimborne BH21 57 D3
Poplar Hill DT11 42 A5
Poppy Cl, Christchurch BH23 29 H2
Poppy Cl, Poole BH16 46 A2
Poppy Way DT6 23 C7
Poppyfields SP8 34 C1
Port Bredy DT6 22 D3
Portchester Ct BH8 21 E3
Portchester Pl BH8 21 E3
Portchester Rd BH8 20 C2
Portesham 13 F4
Portfield Cl BH23 28 A3
Portfield Rd BH23 28 A3
Portland Beach Rd DT5 32 A1
Portland Castle (EH) DT5 32 B1
Portland Cres DT4 54 C2
Portland Ct DT7 35 C3
Portland Hospital DT5 32 B1
Portland Museum DT5 33 E7
Portland Rd DT4 54 C4
Portman Dr DT11 42 C1
Portman Mews BH7 21 H3
Portman Pl DT11 19 A4
Portman Rd, Blandford Forum DT11 18 A2
Portman Rd, Bournemouth BH7 21 H3
Portmore Gdns DT4 55 E3
Portwey Cl DT4 55 E3
Post Green Rd BH16 37 B2
Post Office Rd BH1 20 B5
Potterne Way BH21 49 D4
Potterne Wood Cl BH31 49 F4
Pottery La DT4 52 C6
Pottery Lines BH20 50 C2
Pound Cl, Dorchester DT2 25 B2
Pound Cl, Sturminster Newton DT10 43 B2
Pound La, Dorchester DT1 31 F3
Pound La, Gillingham SP8 34 A2
Pound La, Lyme Regis DT7 35 B1
Pound La, Poole BH15 38 C2
Pound La, Shaftesbury SP7 40 D3
Pound La, Wareham BH20 50 B6
Pound Piece, Dorchester DT2 37 C5
Pound Piece, Portland DT5 33 C6
Pound Rd DT7 35 D3
Pound St DT7 35 D3
Poundbury 13 G3
Poundbury Cres DT1 30 C3
Poundbury Rd DT2 30 A1
Poundbury West Ind Est DT1 30 D2
Powerstock 13 E2
Powys Cl DT1 30 C5
Powys Grn DT9 41 C3
Powys La DT9 41 C3
Poxwell 13 H4
Preetz Way DT11 19 D2
Prescombe Down NNR 10 D3
Prestleigh 9 F1
Preston 13 G4
Preston Beach Rd DT3 53 F3
Preston Cl BH16 46 D2
Preston Ct BH20 50 B4
Preston Rd, Poole BH15 38 B1
Preston Rd, Weymouth DT3 53 G2
Pretoria Ter DT4 54 D3
Priestlands Cnr*, Priestlands La DT9 41 D2
Priestlands DT9 41 C2
Priestlands La DT9 41 C2
Priest's House (NT) 8 C3
Priests House Museum & Garden BH21 57 B3
Priests Mews BH19 45 F4
Priests Rd BH19 45 E4
Priests Way BH19 44 C5
Primrose Cl SP8 34 B2
Primrose Way, Christchurch BH23 29 H2
Primrose Way, Wimborne BH21 27 C1
Primula Cl DT3 48 D6
Prince Consort Walk DT5 32 E1
Prince of Wales Rd, Dorchester DT1 31 E4

Russell Gdns BH16 47 B1
Russell-Cotes Art Gallery & Museum BH1 20 C6
Russett Gdns DT6 22 E2
Rutland Rd DT4 54 D1
Rutter Cl SP7 40 D3
Ryall 12 C2
Ryan Bsns Pk BH20 50 C4
Ryan Cl BH20 50 B4
Ryan Ct DT11 19 B4
Rye Hill BH20 17 B3
Rye Hill Cl BH20 17 C3
Ryemead La DT4 54 C6
Rylands La DT4 54 C4
Rymbury DT3 39 C2
Ryme Intrinseca 9 F5

S

Sable Ct BH5 21 G4
Saffron Dr BH23 29 H2
St Alban St DT4 55 F2
St Albans Av BH8 20 D1
St Albans Rd BH8 20 D1
St Aldhelm's Chapel 14 C5
St Aldhelms Rd DT9 41 D1
St Andrews Av DT3 52 D3
St Andrews Church, East Lulworth 14 A4
St Andrews Cl DT1 31 G5
St Andrews Cres DT6 22 D2
St Andrews Dr DT6 25 B5
St Andrews Gdns DT6 22 E2
St Andrews Ind Est DT6 22 E2
St Andrews Mdw DT7 35 C3
St Andrews Rd, Bridport DT6 22 D3
St Andrews Rd, Broadstone BH18 27 F3
St Andrews Ter*, St Andrews Gdns DT6 22 E2
St Andrews Well DT6 22 E2
St Annes Rd, Poole BH16 46 C2
St Annes Rd, Weymouth DT4 54 D5
St Anns Ct*, Palmerston Mews BH1 21 G3
St Anthonys Rd BH2 20 B3
St Antonys Sq DT9 41 D4
St Aubyns Ct BH15 38 A5
St Augustins Rd BH2 20 B2
St Candida 12 C2
St Catherines BH21 57 C4
St Catherine's Chapel 13 E4
St Catherines Cres DT9 41 B3
St Catherines Way DT9 41 B3
St Cecilias Gdns DT6 22 C2
St Clements Gdns BH1 21 F3
St Clements La BH15 38 A6
St Clements Rd BH1 21 F3
St Cuthburga 14 D1
St Davids Cl DT1 31 G5
St Davids Ct*, Palmerston Mews BH1 21 G3
St Davids Rd, Poole BH16 46 C2
St Davids Rd, Weymouth DT4 54 D5
St Edwards Cl, Shaftesbury SP7 40 D2
St Edwards Cl, Wareham BH20 26 C5
St Edwards Ct SP7 40 D3
St Georges Av DT4 53 E4
St Georges Cl, Dorchester DT1 31 H4
St Georges Cl, Swanage BH19 44 A4
St Georges Ct BH1 21 G3
St Georges Est Rd DT5 33 B6
St Georges Hill DT7 35 C2
St Georges Rd, Dorchester DT1 31 G3
St Georges Rd, Portland DT5 33 C6
St Georges Rd, Shaftesbury SP7 40 D3
St Gregory'S Church 9 H4
St Helens Rd, Dorchester DT1 30 D3
St Helens Rd, Wareham BH20 50 D1
St Helier Av DT3 48 A4
St Hellens Rd DT4 54 A2
St Ives 15 E1
St Ives Gdns BH2 20 C3
St James Cl BH15 38 A6
St James DT8 16 A5
St James Pk DT6 22 F1
St James Pl DT1 30 D4
St James St SP7 40 B4
St James's Common SP7 40 B4
St John The Baptist BH20 17 B2
St Johns Cl, Portland DT5 32 C3
St Johns Cl, Wimborne BH21 57 C4
St Johns Ct*, Palmerston Mews BH1 21 G3
St Johns Hill, Shaftesbury SP7 40 B3
St Johns Hill, Wareham BH20 50 B6
St Johns Hill, Wimborne BH21 57 C3
St Johns Rd, Bournemouth BH5 21 G4
St Johns Rd, Christchurch BH23 28 A4
St Johns Rd, Poole BH15 38 C3
St Julien Cres DT3 48 A5
St Julien Rd BH20 24 B4
St Katherines Av DT6 22 D3
St Katherines Dr DT6 22 E2
St Lawrence Cres SP7 40 D2
St Lawrence Rd DT3 48 A3
St Lawrence*, Church St DT6 24 B2
St Ledgers Pl BH8 21 F2
St Ledgers Rd BH8 21 F1
St Leonards 15 E1
St Leonards Av DT11 19 C4
St Leonards Ct DT11 19 C4
St Leonards Rd, Bournemouth BH8 20 D2
St Leonards Rd, Weymouth DT4 55 E3
St Leonards Ter DT11 19 D3
St Lukes Ct DT6 22 A2
St Lukes Rd BH3 20 B1
St Margarets Almshouses BH21 57 A2
St Margarets Av BH23 28 A5
St Margarets Church, East Wellow 11 H4
St Margarets Cl BH21 57 A2
St Margarets Hill BH21 57 A2
St Margarets Rd BH15 38 C3
St Martins Cl, Dorchester DT2 17 B6
St Martins Cl, Wareham BH20 50 B5
St Martins La, Shaftesbury SP7 40 C3
St Martins La, Wareham BH20 50 B5
St Martins Pl BH20 50 D1
St Martins Rd, Poole BH16 46 B2
St Martins Rd, Portland DT5 32 C3
St Martins Rd, Wareham BH20 50 D1
St Martins Rd, Weymouth DT4 54 D4
St Martins Sq SP8 34 C3
St Mary St DT4 55 F2
St Mary Well St DT8 16 B6
St Marys Cl BH20 50 A4
St Marys Ct SP8 34 C3
St Marys Gdns DT8 16 A5
St Marys Pl DT6 22 C4
St Marys Rd, Bournemouth BH1 21 F2
St Marys Rd, Poole BH15 38 C4
St Marys Rd, Sherbourne DT9 41 B4
St Michaels Bsns Centre* Church St DT7 35 E3
St Michaels Cl, Poole BH15 47 D3
St Michaels Cl, Verwood BH31 49 C3
St Michaels Cl, Weymouth DT4 54 D3
St Michaels Gdns DT7 35 D3
St Michaels La DT6 22 B3
St Michaels Mew*, West Hill Rd BH2 20 A5
St Michaels Pl*, West Hill Rd BH2 20 A5
St Michaels Rd, Bournemouth BH2 20 A5
St Michaels Rd, Verwood BH31 49 C3
St Michaels Rd, Wareham BH20 50 B6
St Michaels Trading Est DT6 22 B4
St Nicholas Ct DT11 42 C2
St Nicholas St DT4 55 F2
St Osmunds Community Sports Centre DT1 31 F5
St Patricks Av DT4 54 A3
St Patricks Ind Est DT11 42 A4
St Pauls Cl DT9 41 D1
St Pauls Grn DT9 41 D1
St Pauls La BH8 20 D4
St Pauls Pl BH8 20 D4
St Pauls Rd, Bournemouth BH8 20 D4
St Pauls Rd, Portland DT5 32 C3
St Peters Cl DT11 18 A1
St Peters Rd BH1 20 C5
St Rumbolds Rd SP7 40 D3
St Stephens La BH31 49 D2
St Stephens Rd BH2 20 B4
St Stephens Way BH2 20 B4
St Swithins Av DT6 22 B3
St Swithins Cl DT9 41 E3
St Swithins Rd, Bridport DT6 22 B3
St Swithins Rd, Sherbourne DT9 41 D3
St Swithuns Rd BH1 21 E4
St Swithuns Rd South BH1 21 E4
St Thomas Ct BH8 20 D3
St Thomas Rd DT1 30 D3
St Thomas St DT4 55 F2
St Valerie Rd BH2 20 B3
St Vast Rd BH19 45 G5
St Winifreds Rd BH2 20 B3
Salerno Pl BH15 47 C4
Salisbury & South Wiltshire Museum 11 F3
Salisbury Cathedral (C of E) 11 F3
Salisbury Cres DT11 19 C3
Salisbury Mews DT1 31 F3
Salisbury Playhouse 11 G3
Salisbury Racecourse 11 E3
Salisbury Rd, Blandford Forum DT11 19 B4
Salisbury Rd, Bournemouth BH1 21 G4
Salisbury Rd, Christchurch BH23 28 D1
Salisbury Rd, Pimperne DT11 18 A3
Salisbury Rd, Shaftesbury SP7 40 D3
Salisbury Rd, Swanage BH19 45 G5
Salisbury Rd, Weymouth DT4 55 E2
Salisbury St, Blandford Forum DT11 19 B4
Salisbury St, Dorchester DT1 31 F3
Salisbury St, Shaftesbury SP7 40 C3
Salisbury Walk DT1 31 F3
Sally Kings La SP7 40 B3
Saltings Rd BH16 46 C3
Salwayash 12 C2
Sammy Miller Museum 15 G2
Samphire Cl DT4 52 D4
Samson Rd BH15 47 C3
San Remo Towers BH5 21 G5
Sandbank 14 D3
Sandbourne Av DT11 19 D2
Sandbourne Cl BH19 44 D5
Sandbourne Rd, Poole BH15 38 C3
Sandbourne Rd, Weymouth DT3 53 G1
Sanderling Cl DT3 48 B4
Sandford 14 C3
Sandford La BH20 50 B4
Sandford La Ind Est BH20 50 C3
Sandford Orcas 9 F4
Sandford Orcas Manor House 9 F4
Sandford Rd, Northport BH20 50 B4
Sandford Rd, Sandford BH20 50 C2
Sandford Ter BH20 50 D1
Sandhills Cres BH20 58 A2
Sandleheath Rd SP6 16 B1
Sandown Rd BH23 29 E4
Sandpit La BH15 38 C4
Sandringham Ct, Bournemouth BH8 21 E2
Sandringham Ct, Dorchester DT1 31 G4
Sandringham Sports Centre DT1 31 G4
Sandy Hill La BH20 26 B4
Sandy Hill Workshops BH20 26 C4
Sandy La, Blandford Forum DT11 42 D1
Sandy La, Poole BH16 46 B3
Sandy La, Verwood BH31 49 D2
Sandy Plot BH23 28 C2
Sarah Sands Cl BH23 28 D2
Sarum Av BH22 56 A2
Sarum St BH15 38 A6
Saville Ct BH21 57 C4
Savoy Ct SP7 40 B3
Sawmills La DT1 31 E5
Saxon Centre BH23 28 B4
Saxon Ct BH20 50 B4
Saxon Mead Cl SP8 34 C1
Saxon Spur SP7 40 D2
Saxon Sq BH23 28 B4
Saxon Way SP6 16 C2
Saxonford Rd BH23 29 H4
Scaplen's Court 14 D3
Schelin Way DT11 42 B6
School Cl*, Jubilee Ct DT1 31 E2
School Cl, Verwood BH31 49 D2
School Cl, Weymouth DT3 26 C1
School Dr, Dorchester DT2 51 B4
School Dr, Sherbourne DT9 41 E2
School Hill DT3 26 B1
School House Cl DT8 16 B5
School La, Blandford Forum DT11 18 A2
School La, Blandford St Mary DT11 19 B6
School La, Dorchester DT1 31 E2
School La, Gillingham SP8 34 D3
School La, Poole BH15 38 B2
School La, Sherbourne DT9 41 C4
School La, West Lulworth BH20 51 C1
School La, Wimborne BH21 57 B2
School Rd SP8 34 D3
School St DT4 55 F1
Scotts Grn BH23 29 F2
Scotts Hills La BH23 28 D4
Scutts Cl BH16 36 C1
Sea Discovery Centre 12 A3
Sea Life Centre DT4 53 F4
Sea Rd BH5 21 G5
Sea Rd North DT6 22 D4
Sea Rd South DT6 23 C6
Sea View Rd BH16 46 B3
Sea Vixen Ind Est BH23 29 F3
Sea Vw DT5 32 B3
Seabank Cl BH16 46 B3
Seaborough 8 C6
Seafield Rd BH23 29 H4
Seagar Way BH15 38 C5
Seamoor Cl DT3 53 F2
Seaton Museum 12 A3
Seaton Tramway 12 A2
Seatown 12 C3
Seaward Ct BH19 45 G2
Seaward Gdns DT6 23 C7
Seaward Rd BH19 45 G2
Seaway Av BH23 29 H3
Second Cliff Walk DT6 23 A8
Sedgefield Cl DT4 54 D2
Sefton Ct BH19 45 G4
Seldown BH15 38 C4
Seldown Bri BH15 38 C5
Seldown La BH15 38 C4
Seldown Rd BH15 38 C4
Seliot Cl BH15 38 C2
Selle Rd BH20 24 C5
Selwood Cl DT10 43 C4
Selwyn Cl DT3 48 C5
Sentry Rd BH19 45 G5
Serpentine La South BH15 38 B4
Serpentine Rd BH15 38 B4
Serrells Mead BH19 44 B4
Seven Acres Rd DT3 39 C2
Seven Barrows Rd BH20 50 A3
Sewell Rd BH20 24 A4
Seymer Cl DT11 42 A4
Seymer Rd BH19 45 H5
Seymour Pl, Bridport DT6 22 D4
Seymour Pl, Wareham BH20 50 B6
Shadow Ct DT11 19 D3
Shadrack DT6 24 B2
Shadrack St DT8 16 B5
Shaftesbury 10 B3
Shaftesbury Abbey, Museum & Gardens SP7 40 B3
Shaftesbury By-Pass SP7 40 B2
Shaftesbury Cl BH22 56 C5
Shaftesbury Ct BH3 20 B2
Shaftesbury Leisure Centre SP7 40 D3
Shaftesbury Rd, Blandford Forum DT11 42 D1
Shaftesbury Rd, Bournemouth BH8 21 E2
Shaftesbury Rd, Ferndown BH22 56 B5
Shaftesbury Rd, Gillingham SP8 34 E4
Shaftesbury Rd, Poole BH15 38 C4
Shaftesbury Town Museum SP7 40 C3
Shakespeare Rd BH21 57 B2
Shapley Ct*, Sherbeton St DT1 30 A3
Shapwick 14 C1
Shapwick Heath NNR 8 C1
Shapwick Rd BH15 47 F4
Shard Cl BH31 49 D2
Sharpitts DT5 33 B6
Shaston Cl BH19 44 D4
Shaston Cres DT1 31 F6
Shatters Hill BH20 50 B5
Shaw Cl DT11 19 B3
Shaw Dr BH20 50 C1
Shears Rd DT4 52 D3
Sheep Market Hill DT11 19 B4
Sheepdown Rd DT1 30 B3
Sheeplands La DT9 41 B3
Shelbourne Rd BH8 20 D1
Sheldrake Rd BH23 29 G5
Shell House 15 F3
Shelley Cl BH1 21 G3
Shelley Gdns BH1 21 G3
Shelley Rd BH1 21 G3
Shelley Rd East BH1 21 H3
Shephards Cl DT11 42 C2
Shepherds Cft DT5 33 E5
Shepherds Way BH20 51 C1
Sheppards Fld BH21 57 B2
Sherbeton St DT1 30 A3
Sherborne 9 F5
Sherborne Abbey DT9 41 D3
Sherborne Castle 9 G5
Sherborne La DT7 35 E3
Sherborne Museum DT9 41 D3
Sherbourne Old Castle (EH) 9 G4
Sherford Cl BH20 50 B3
Sherford Dr BH20 50 B3
Sheridan Imax Cinema BH2 20 C6
Sherren Cotts DT2 17 C6
Sherrin Cl BH15 38 C2
Sherwood Cl BH23 28 A3
Sherwood Dr BH31 49 E2
Shetland Vw BH31 49 D2
Shillingstone 10 A6
Shillingstone La DT11 42 A5
Shipstal Cl BH16 47 B1
Shipton Gorge 12 D3

Shipton La DT6 24 B2
Shire La DT7 35 B3
Shirecroft Rd DT4 54 C1
Shires Mead BH31 49 D2
Shirley Cl, Ferndown BH22 56 B4
Shirley Cl, Swanage BH19 45 E4
Shirley Ct DT1 30 D4
Shirley Rd, Poole BH16 46 C2
Shirley Rd, Wareham BH20 50 A6
Shoe La DT6 22 E2
Shooters La SP7 40 C3
Shooters Pad SP7 40 C3
Shore Av BH16 46 D4
Shore Cl BH16 46 D4
Shore Gdns BH16 46 C4
Shore La BH16 46 C4
Shore Rd BH19 45 G2
Short Rd DT4 54 D1
Shortedge DT10 43 C4
Shortlands DT5 33 C6
Shortlands Rd DT3 48 A3
Shortmoor DT8 16 C4
Shorts Cl BH23 28 C1
Shorts La, Beaminster DT8 16 B5
Shorts La, Blandford Forum DT11 19 B4
Shottesford Av DT11 19 D1
Shottsford Cl BH19 44 D4
Shottsford Rd BH15 38 B1
Shreen Cl SP8 34 D2
Shreen Way SP8 34 D1
Shroton 10 B5
Shrubbery La DT4 54 B5
Sidmouth Rd DT7 35 A4
Signals Av DT11 19 D2
Silchester Cl BH2 20 B3
Silk House Barton DT10 43 B1
Silton 9 H3
Silver Bsns Pk BH23 29 F3
Silver St, Christchurch BH23 28 B4
Silver St, Lyme Regis DT7 35 D3
Silver St, Weymouth DT3 39 D1
Silverdale Cl BH18 27 D4
Silverdale Cres SP6 16 C2
Silverwood Cl BH21 57 D6
Simene Cl DT6 22 A3
Simene Walk SP8 34 F4
Simmonds Cl BH15 38 C2
Simons Rd DT9 41 D1
Sir Richard Hull Rd BH20 24 A5
Sitterton BH20 17 A2
Sitterton Cl BH20 17 B1
Sixpenny Handley 10 D5
Sk8 Park DT4 53 F4
Skilling Hill Rd DT6 23 A5
Skilling La DT6 23 B5
Skinner St BH15 38 B6
Slades Grn DT6 23 D5
Sleepbrook Cl BH31 49 B2
Slepe 14 C2
Slinn Rd BH23 29 E3
Slip Way BH15 38 A5
Slough La BH16 37 D2
Slyers La DT2 31 G2
Smoky Hole La DT1 31 G4
Smugglers Reach BH23 29 G6
Snakey La SP7 40 C3
Snow Down Rd DT11 18 B6
Snow Hill BH20 17 B2
Snow Hill La BH20 17 C2
Snowdrop Gdns BH23 29 H2
Soberton Rd BH8 21 F1
Sodern La DT2 25 A2
Solent Meads Par Three Golf Club BH6 28 B6
Solent Rd BH19 45 G6
Solomon Way BH15 47 D3
Somerby Rd BH15 38 C1
Somerfields DT7 35 C3
Somerford Av BH23 29 G2
Somerford Bsns Pk BH23 29 F3
Somerford Rd BH23 29 E4
Somerford Way BH23 29 E4
Somerleigh Ct DT1 31 E3
Somerleigh Gate DT1 31 E3
Somerleigh Rd DT1 31 E3
Somers Rd DT7 35 C3
Somerset Brick & Tile Museum 8 A1
Somerset Cl SP8 34 C2
Somerset Rd, Bournemouth BH7 21 H3
Somerset Rd, Weymouth DT4 54 C1
Somerset Rural Life Museum 8 D1
Somerville Rd BH2 20 A5
Sopers La BH23 28 A5
Sopwith Cl BH23 29 H4
Sopwith Cres BH21 57 D6
Sorrel Cl DT4 53 E4
Sorrel Way SP8 34 A2
Sorrell Ct BH23 29 G2
Sorrell Way BH23 29 G2
Souter Way DT3 52 D2
South Annings DT6 24 B2
South Av, Lyme Regis DT7 35 D2
South Av, Sherbourne DT9 41 B4
South Causeway BH20 50 B6
South Chard 12 B1
South Cliffe Rd BH19 45 G6
South Court Av DT1 31 E5
South Cres DT11 18 C4
South Ct DT9 41 B4
South Dro DT2 17 A6
South Haven Cl BH16 47 A2
South Hill SP6 16 C2
South Lawns DT6 23 D5
South Mead BH20 17 B2
South Mill La DT6 22 C4
South Par DT4 55 F2
South Pk DT4 26 D3
South Rd, Bournemouth BH1 20 C6
South Rd, Poole BH15 38 B5
South Rd, Springbourne BH1 21 G3
South Rd, S wanage BH19 45 E4
South Rd, Weymouth DT4 54 B6
South Rd, Wimborne BH21 27 C1
South St, Bridport DT6 22 C4
South St, Dorchester DT1 31 E3
South St, Gillingham SP8 34 C3
South St, Sherbourne DT9 41 D3
South St, Wareham BH20 50 B6
South View Pl BH2 20 A5
South View Rd BH23 28 A4
South Vw DT2 17 C6
South Walk DT6 22 C4
South Walks DT1 31 E3
South Walks Rd DT1 31 E4
South Western Bsns Pk DT9 41 D4
Southbourne 15 F3
Southbrook BH20 17 B2
Southcliffe Rd BH23 29 H4
Southcote Ho BH1 21 F3
Southcote Rd BH1 21 E4
Southcroft Rd DT4 54 B3
Southdown Av DT3 53 F2
Southdown Rd DT4 54 D5
Southdown Way BH22 56 B5
Southern Av BH22 56 C5
Southernhay Rd BH31 49 E2
Southey Rd BH23 29 F2
Southfield Av DT4 52 D4
Southfield La DT11 42 B3
Southill Garden Dr DT4 52 B4
Southlands 13 G5
Southlands Av BH21 27 C2
Southlands Cl BH21 27 C2
Southlands Ct BH18 27 F4
Southlands Rd DT4 55 E4
Southover Cl DT11 19 B6
Southover DT6 24 B3
Southview Rd DT4 54 D1
Southwell 13 G6
Southwell Rd DT5 33 D7
Sovereign Bsns Pk BH15 38 A1
Sovereign Centre BH1 21 G3
Spa Av DT3 52 C3
Spa Rd DT3 52 B3
Sparacre Gdns DT6 22 C3
Sparrow Cft SP8 34 F4
Speedwell Dr BH23 29 G2
Spencer Gdns DT11 42 C6
Spencer Rd BH1 21 E4
Spetisbury 14 B1
Spetisbury Rings 14 B1
Spiller Rd DT3 26 B2
Spinners Cl BH22 56 A5
Spinning Way DT6 22 C4
Spitfire Cl DT2 51 B5
Spittles La DT7 35 E2
Spring Av DT4 55 F3
Spring Cl, Bridport DT6 22 E1
Spring Cl, Verwood BH31 49 C3
Spring Gdns, Dorchester DT2 17 C5
Spring Gdns, Portland DT5 32 C3
Spring Gdns, Weymouth DT4 55 E3
Spring La DT4 55 F3
Spring Rd, Bournemouth BH1 21 E3
Spring Rd, Weymouth DT4 55 F3
Spring St BH20 58 D2
Springdale Av BH18 27 E3
Springdale Gro BH21 27 C4
Springdale Rd BH21 27 B4
Springfield Cl, Shaftesbury SP7 40 D1
Springfield Cl, Verwood BH31 49 C3
Springfield Cres, Sherbourne DT9 41 B4
Springfield Cres, Weymouth DT3 48 A5
Springfield Mews*, Portmore Gdns DT4 55 E3
Springfield Mews*, Springfield Rd BH19 45 G4
Springfield Rd, Swanage BH19 45 G4
Springfield Rd, Verwood BH31 49 B3
Springfield Rd, Weymouth DT3 48 A5
Springfields DT10 43 C2
Springfld Av BH6 28 A6
Springham Walk DT1 30 C3
Springhead Rd DT7 35 B1
Springhill Gdns DT7 35 D2
Springhill*, Springfield Rd BH19 45 G4
Springrove BH20 17 C2
Springwater Dr BH23 28 D4
Springwell Cl BH20 26 B5
Spy Cl BH16 36 B2
Squirrel Vw BH20 24 B5
Squirrel Walk BH31 49 C3
Stadium Way BH15 38 B4
Stafford Cl DT2 17 C4
Stafford Mews*, Stafford Rd BH19 45 G4
Stafford Rd, Bournemouth BH1 20 D4
Stafford Rd, Swanage BH19 45 G5
Stagswood BH31 49 A2
Stainforth Cl DT4 54 B1
Stair Hole BH20 51 B3
Stalbridge 9 H4
Stalbridge Cl DT10 43 C2
Stalbridge La DT10 43 A4
Stalbridge Weston 9 H5
Stanbarrow Cl BH20 17 B2
Stanbridge 14 D1
Standfast Walk DT1 31 F5
Stanforth Ct BH23 28 C4
Stanier Rd DT3 39 B2
Stanley Barracks BH20 24 A6
Stanley Cl BH31 49 D3
Stanley Ct BH15 38 B1
Stanley DT4 52 D6
Stanley Green Cres BH15 38 B2
Stanley Green Ind Est BH15 38 B2
Stanley Green Rd BH15 38 B2
Stanley Rd, Bournemouth BH1 21 E3
Stanley Rd, Poole BH15 38 B6
Stanley Sq DT11 18 D5
Stanpit BH23 28 D4
Stanpit Marsh Nature Reserve BH23 28 D6
Stanstead Rd DT2 37 C5
Stanton Cl DT11 19 C3
Stanton Ct DT4 53 E5
Stapehill 15 E1
Stapehill Abbey & Gardens 15 E1
Staplecross La BH23 28 D2
Staples Ter DT7 35 E2
Starlight Farm Cl BH31 49 D2
Station App, Broadstone BH18 27 F4
Station App, Dorchester DT1 31 E4
Station Cotts DT2 51 D4
Station Ct DT11 19 C4
Station Pl BH19 45 G4
Station Rd Bsns Pk DT10 43 D1
Station Rd Ind Est DT2 37 C5
Station Rd, Alderholt SP6 16 B2
Station Rd, Child Okeford DT11 42 C3
Station Rd, Christchurch BH23 28 A3
Station Rd, Dorchester DT2 51 C5
Station Rd, Ferndown BH22 56 A2
Station Rd, Gillingham SP8 34 D4
Station Rd, Maiden Newton DT2 37 C5
Station Rd, Poole BH15 47 F4
Station Rd, Portland DT5 33 C6
Station Rd, Sherbourne DT9 41 D4
Station Rd, Shillingstone DT11 42 A4
Station Rd, Stalbridge DT10 43 C2
Station Rd, Sturminster Newton DT10 43 B6
Station Rd, Swanage BH19 45 G4
Station Rd, Verwood BH31 49 A1
Station Rd, West Bay DT6 23 B8
Station Rd, Wimborne BH21 57 C4
Station Rd, Wool BH20 58 C2
Station Ter BH21 57 C4
Station Yd SP6 16 A2
Staverton Walk DT11 19 B3
Stavordale Ct DT4 55 E1
Stavordale Rd DT4 55 E1
Steeple 14 B4
Steeple Cl DT3 52 B2
Steer Rd BH19 45 E4
Stembridge Tower Mill (NT) 8 C2
Stenhurst Rd BH15 38 D1
Stephens Castle Nature Reserve BH31 49 D1
Stepnell Reach BH16 46 D4
Steppes BH19 44 B4
Steppes Hill BH19 44 B4
Sterte Av BH15 38 B3
Sterte Av West BH15 38 A3
Sterte Cl BH15 38 B3
Sterte Ct BH15 38 B3
Sterte Esp BH15 38 B3
Sterte Ind Est BH15 38 A3
Sterte Rd BH15 38 B3
Stevens Cl DT11 19 C2
Stevenson Cl BH21 57 C4
Stevensons Ct DT6 22 C4
Stewart Cl BH8 21 E3
Stewart Mews BH8 21 E3
Stewart Rd BH8 20 D2
Stickland Ct DT11 19 B5
Stile La DT7 35 D4
Stinsford 13 G3
Stinsford Hill DT2 31 G2
Stinsford Vw DT1 31 G4
Stirling Rd, Bournemouth BH3 20 B1
Stirling Rd, Weymouth DT3 52 C2
Stirling Way BH23 29 G4
Stirrup Cl BH16 46 E2
Stoborough 14 B4
Stoborough Cl DT3 52 B2
Stoborough Green 14 B4
Stoborough Heath NNR 14 C4
Stockley Rd BH20 50 A3
Stoke Abbott 12 D1
Stoke Rd, Beaminster DT8 16 A6
Stoke Rd, Weymouth DT4 54 C6
Stoke Wood Rd BH3 20 B2
Stokeford 14 B3
Stokehouse St DT1 30 B4
Stokes Av BH15 38 B3
Stoke-sub-Hamdon Priory (NT) 8 D5
Stone La BH21 57 A2
Stone La Ind Est BH21 57 A2
Stonebarrow La DT6 25 D5
Stonechat Cl DT3 48 B4
Stonechat Ct BH23 29 E3
Stonedene DT9 41 D1
Stonehenge (EH) 11 E1
Stonehill Ct DT4 54 B5
Stoney Pth SP7 40 B3
Stony La BH23 28 C1
Stony La South BH23 28 C4
Story La BH18 27 F4
Stottingway St DT3 48 A3
Stour Cl DT11 42 B6
Stour Ct SP8 34 B2
Stour Dr BH20 50 B3
Stour Gdns SP8 34 C3
Stour Mdws SP8 34 B4
Stour Mews DT10 43 B6
Stour Pk DT11 19 C6
Stour Provost 10 A4
Stour Rd, Blandford Forum DT11 19 C5
Stour Rd, Bournemouth BH8 21 F2
Stour Rd, Christchurch BH23 28 A5
Stour Row 10 A4
Stour View Cl DT10 43 B4
Stour Walk*, Eden Gro BH21 57 C4
Stourbank Rd BH23 28 A4
Stourcastle Cl SP8 34 C1
Stourhead (NT) 9 H2
Stourpaine 10 B6
Stourton Caundle 9 G5
Stourton House Garden 9 H2
Stowcastle St DT1 30 B4
Stowell Cres BH20 50 A6
Stowey St DT1 30 B3
Straits DT5 33 D6
Strand St BH15 38 B6
Strathmore Dr BH31 49 D2
Stratton 13 G2
Streche Rd, Swanage BH19 45 G1
Streche Rd, Wareham BH20 50 B5
Strete Mt BH23 29 E3
Stroud Gdns BH23 29 E4
Stroud La BH23 29 E4
Stroud Park Av BH23 29 E4
Stroudley Cres DT3 39 C2
Stuart Cl BH16 46 C2
Stuart La SP8 34 B3
Stuart Way DT6 22 E3
Stubhampton 10 C5
Studland 14 D4
Studland & Godlingston Heath NNR 14 D4
Studland Way DT3 52 B2
Study Gallery 14 D3
Sturminster Marshall 14 C1
Sturminster Newton 9 H5
Sturminster Newton Leisure Centre DT10 43 C4
Sturminster Newton Museum DT10 43 B4
Sturminster Rd SP7 40 B4
Styles Cl DT8 16 B4
Styles La DT2 39 B5
Sudan Rd DT4 55 E4
Suffolk Rd BH2 20 A5
Suffolk Rd South BH2 20 A4
Summer Flds BH31 49 B4
Summercroft Way BH22 56 B4
Summerhill Rd DT7 35 E2
Summers La BH23 28 D1

74

Red Books *showing the way*

For the latest publication list, prices and to order online please visit our website.

LOCAL STREET ATLASES

Abingdon, Didcot
Aldershot, Camberley
Alfreton, Belper
Andover
Ashford, Tenterden
Aylesbury, Tring
Bangor, Caernarfon
Barnstaple, Bideford
Basildon, Billericay
Basingstoke, Alton
Bath, Bradford-on-Avon
Bedford
Bodmin, Wadebridge
Bournemouth
Bracknell
Brentwood
Brighton
Bristol
Bromley
Burton upon Trent
Bury Saint Edmunds, Stowmarket
Cambridge
Cannock, Rugeley
Cardiff
Carlisle, Penrith
Chelmsford, Braintree
Chester, Wrexham
Chesterfield, Dronfield
Chichester, Bognor Regis
Chippenham, Calne
Coatbridge, Airdrie
Colchester, Clacton-on-Sea
Corby, Kettering, Wellingborough
Coventry, Rugby
Crawley, Mid-Sussex
Crewe, Nantwich
Derby
Dundee, Saint Andrews
Eastbourne, Hailsham
Edinburgh
Exeter, Exmouth
Falkirk, Grangemouth
Fareham, Gosport
Flintshire Towns
Folkestone, Dover
Glasgow
Gloucester, Cheltenham
Gravesend, Dartford
Grays, Thurrock
Great Yarmouth, Lowestoft
Grimsby, Cleethorpes
Guildford, Woking
Hamilton, Motherwell
Harlow, Bishops Stortford
Harrogate, Knaresborough
Hastings, Bexhill
Hereford
Hertford, Waltham Cross
High Wycombe
Huntingdon, Saint Neots
Ipswich
Isle of Man
Isle of Wight
Kendal, Windermere
Kidderminster, Stourport-on-Severn
Kingston upon Hull
Lancaster, Morecambe
Leicester
Lincoln, Washingborough
Llandudno, Colwyn Bay
Loughborough, Coalville
Luton, Dunstable
Macclesfield, Wilmslow
Maidstone
Mansfield, Sutton in Ashfield
Medway, Gillingham
Mid Wales Towns
Milton Keynes
New Forest
Newark-on-Trent
Newbury, Thatcham
Newport, Chepstow
Newquay, Perranporth
Northampton
Northwich, Winsford
Norwich

Nottingham
Nuneaton, Bedworth
Oxford, Kidlington
Penzance, Saint Ives
Perth, Kinross
Peterborough, Stamford
Plymouth
Portsmouth
Reading, Henley-on-Thames
Redditch, Kidderminster
Reigate, Mole Valley
Rhyl, Prestatyn
Rugby
Saint Albans, Welwyn, Hatfield
Saint Austell, Lostwithiel
Salisbury, Wilton
Scarborough, Whitby
Scunthorpe
Sevenoaks
Shrewsbury
Sittingbourne, Faversham
Slough, Maidenhead, Windsor
Solihull
Southampton
Southend-on-Sea
Stafford
Stevenage, Letchworth
Stirling, Alloa
Stoke-on-Trent
Stroud, Nailsworth
Swansea
Swindon, Chippenham
Tamworth, Lichfield
Taunton, Bridgwater
Telford, Newport
Tenby, Saundersfoot
Thanet, Canterbury
Torbay, Newton Abbot
Trowbridge, Frome
Truro, Falmouth
Tunbridge Wells, Tonbridge
Walsall
Warwick, Royal Leamington Spa
Watford, Hemel Hempstead
Wells, Glastonbury
West Midlands, Birmingham
Weston-super-Mare
Weymouth, Dorchester
Winchester
Worcester
Workington, Whitehaven
Worthing, Littlehampton
Wrexham
York

COUNTY STREET ATLASES
(Town Centre Maps)

Bedfordshire
Berkshire
Buckinghamshire
Cambridgeshire
Cheshire
Cornwall
Cumbria
Derbyshire
Devon
Dorset
East Sussex
Essex
Gloucestershire
Hampshire
Herefordshire
Hertfordshire
Kent
Leicestershire, Rutland
Lincolnshire
Norfolk
Northamptonshire
Nottinghamshire
Oxfordshire
Shropshire
Somerset
Staffordshire
Suffolk
Surrey
Warwickshire
West Sussex

Wiltshire
Worcestershire

EUROPEAN STREET MAPS

Calais & Boulogne Shoppers Map (Sheet Map)
Dieppe Shoppers Map (Sheet Map)
North French Towns Street Atlas

LEISURE & TOURIST MAPS

Argyll & The Isles
Argyll, The Isles, Loch Lomond, Stirling & Trossachs
British Isles
Caithness & Sutherland
Chilterns & Thames Valley
Cornwall
Cotswolds & Severn Valley
Dartmoor & South Devon Coast
Devon
Devon & Cornwall
Dorset & The Channel Islands
East Anglia
Edinburgh & The Lothians
England & Wales
Exmoor & North Devon Coast
Fife (Kingdom of)
Fort William, Ben Nevis & Glen Coe
Grampian Highlands & Aberdeen
Great Britain
Greater Glasgow & Clyde Valley
Greater London (M25)
Heart of Scotland
Highlands of Scotland
Historic Scotland
Iona & Mull
Isle of Arran
Isle of Man
Isle of Man (Deluxe)
Isle of Wight
Kent & East Sussex
Kent to Cornwall
Lake District
Loch Lomond
Loch Ness & Aviemore
North Pennines & Lakes
North West England
North York Moors
Orkney & Shetland Islands
Outer Hebrides
Peak District
Perthshire
Scotland
Scotland (Atlas)
Scotland (Homelands of the Clans)
Shetland & Orkney Islands
Skye & Lochalsh
Snowdonia
South East England
South East England
Southern England
Surrey & Sussex Downs
Sussex
The Cotswolds
The Mid Shires
The Shires of Middle England
Wales
Wales (Atlas)
Wessex
Yorkshire
Yorkshire Dales

EUROPEAN LEISURE MAPS

Belgium, Luxembourg & Netherlands
Cross Channel Visitors Map
Europe
France & Belgium
Germany
Ireland
Italy
Spain & Portugal

WORLD MAPS

World Map - Political
World Travel Adventure Map

RED BOOKS (ESTATE PUBLICATIONS) Ltd, Bridewell House, Tenterden, Kent. TN30 6EP
Tel: 01580 764225   Fax: 01580 763720   Email: sales@redbooks-maps.co.uk